The Hippo That Fell Off the Seesaw

and

Other Parables from Christian Counseling

Rita Huang

Ph.D., Psy.D,. M.A., M.Ed., B.A.

Published by
Innovo Publishing LLC
www.innovopublishing.com
1-888-546-2111

Providing Full-Service Publishing Services for
Christian Authors, Artists, and Organizations: Hardbacks, Paperbacks,
eBooks, Audiobooks, Music, and Videos.

THE HIPPO THAT FELL OFF THE SEESAW
AND OTHER PARABLES FROM CHRISTIAN COUNSELING

Copyright © 2011 Rita Huang
All rights reserved.

No part of this publication may be reproduced, stored in a retrieval system,
or transmitted in any form or by any means electronic, mechanical, photocopying,
recording, or otherwise, without the prior written permission of the copyright holders.

All character names and locations of the following stories have been changed.

All Scripture quotes are from the Women's Devotional Bible,
New International Version by Zondervan Publishing House. Copyright © 1990, 1994.

Library of Congress Number: 2011935185
ISBN 13: 978-1-936076-97-0
ISBN 10: 1-936076-97-7

Cover Design & Interior Layout by Innovo Publishing LLC

Printed in the United States of America
U.S. Printing History
First Edition: September 2011

ACKNOWLEDGMENTS

First of all, I would like to thank my Lord, Jesus Christ, who gave me the insight to write this book. I truly have experienced God's presence and faithfulness throughout the whole process.

I would also like to thank all my patients and friends who inspired and encouraged me to complete the book. Without them, it would not have been published.

I would like to acknowledge my husband, Raywin, for his love, encouragement, and technical support.

I also thank my children, Ritchie and Rachelle, and their spouses, Grace and Michael, for their inspiration, encouragement, wisdom, love, and support. Being their mother has been a great source of joy, fulfillment, and pride.

I thank my editor, Mary Frances Moore, for contributing her editorial expertise. This book would not have been published without her help and support.

Lastly, I would like to thank my parents for their unfailing love for me. Watching them struggle when I was a child taught me to have compassion for those who are hurting. God has turned my wounds into blessing by using me to help those who are struggling emotionally. I see God's miracles performed in people's lives daily as He turns impossible situations into possible. It gives me so much joy to see people's facial expressions turn from anger and hurt into joy and encouragement. Most of all, the greatest joy for me is to see my patients turn to God for answers. May the Lord use this book to make a difference in your life as you read it.

CONTENTS

CHALLENGES/CRISES IN LIFE 7
    CAN TREESTONE SURVIVE? 9
    GIANT TRUCK 13
    THE LITTLE SPARROW 21
    SMALL VOICE IN A NOISY ROOM 25

CHRISTIAN LIVING 31
    BIKE RIDING WITHOUT THE TRAINING WHEELS 33
    BOOMERANG 37
    ERASABLE CARDBOARD PAD 40
    FARMER JACK 41
    THE HEADLIGHT 45
    PASS THE MESSAGE GAME 49
    THE SQUIRREL 52
    THE WINDSHIELD AND THE REARVIEW MIRROR 57

COPING MECHANISM 61
    GLASSES 63
    THE GRAY ZONE 67
    A RED PUNCHING BAG 72
    WHITE WALL AND BLUE DOTS 75

CONFLICTS 81
    THE COW 83
    THE CRACKED FLOWER VASE 87
    FROM FINGER POINTING, TO A CLENCHED FIST,
        TO AN OPEN HAND 89
    MR. PAINTER & MRS. POINTER 93
    THE "POOP" FAUCET 97
    THE TRAIN ON THE TRAIN TRACK 101

EMOTIONAL DISTURBANCE 105

    CONQUERING THE CREATURES: AN ARCADE GAME 107
    HOW MANY BACKPACKS DO YOU WANT TO CARRY? 111
    THE HEALING POWER OF WILLOW 117
    ROLLER COASTER RIDE 121
    THE TWILIGHT ZONE 126
    UMBRELLA 128
    WHAT ABOUT BOB? 131

RELATIONSHIPS 135

    THE BAND-AID RELATIONSHIP 137
    CELL PHONE 140
    FROZEN OR MELTING MOMENTS 144
    THE HIPPO THAT FELL OFF THE SEESAW 148
    HOLES IN THE BUCKET 150
    MR. GREEN SQUARE & MISS GREEN CIRCLE 153
    PAPER PLATE AND CHINA PLATE 158
    OVERLAPPING CIRCLES: A VIDEO GAME 163
    HOW BIG IS YOUR PIECE OF THE PIE? 167
    THE PUSHY BULLDOZER AND WIMPY SOIL 173
    TURTLE PEOPLE 176
    RELATIONAL CIRCLE 179

SELF-IMAGE/SELF-ESTEEM 183

    GROUP PHOTO 185
    MIRROR, MIRROR ON THE WALL 187
    THE SENSITIVE PLANT (MIMOSA PUDICA) 191

CHALLENGES/CRISES IN LIFE

CAN TREESTONE SURVIVE?

Once upon a time, there was an old oak tree in an empty lot near a small village. Sky-high and perfectly formed, it seemed invincible because for over one hundred years it had weathered droughts, floods, and all types of storms. Numerous birds and squirrels made their homes in its lofty branches, and children played in the coolness of its shade. Sometimes winter hoarfrost covered its bark, and when lit by the sun's rays, it sparkled as if it were covered with a million diamonds.

So beautiful, so majestic was this mighty oak that the townsfolk fondly named it Treestone. The citizens voted to turn the empty lot into a park with benches, a picnic table, and a drinking fountain. The proudest moment of all came when a sign was erected telling about the tree and the history of the town. This tree was indeed very special to the little community.

Late one frigid, spring night, a truck filled with teenagers slammed head-on into the tree, killing the driver and injuring several others. Within minutes, screaming sirens ripped through the dead of night, sending a terrifying message to everyone that all was not well. People rushed out to see what had happened. On the scene were ambulances, fire trucks, and police cars; onlookers, relatives and friends. There was much crying and wailing as everyone tried to make sense out of that which made no sense.

After the ambulances raced off to the hospital and everyone had left, the park seemed eerily quiet and, as was usual for that time of the night, Treestone was alone and everything was different. The attention had been diverted mainly to the teens and no one paid much attention to the terrible damage done to Treestone, and to the park itself.

The force of the truck's impact had split Treestone's trunk wide open and sent one of its huge limbs crashing to the ground. As it fell, it had smashed the treasured historical sign into fragments, leaving shattered and splintered boards everywhere. There were also deep ruts in the ground from where the trucks and ambulances had driven.

The town mourned the lost driver, for those who were hurt, and for the families of everyone involved. They also mourned their beloved Treestone. Village workers spent many hours restoring the park and the sign, hauling in dirt, and grading it just right. They even erected a little cross and planted flowers in memory of the lives lost. That summer, Treestone produced no buds on its branches. The split trunk had left the tree vulnerable to insects and disease. Everyone wondered if this beloved tree would survive. Throughout the summer people watched for some sign of life, but there was none to be found.

In one fell swoop, the entire town had been changed forever.

The following spring, Tom, a friend of the boy who was killed, went to the park to sit and think, to ponder and to pray. He sat on the park bench and contemplated the events of that life-changing night—of the losses—and he asked himself if there had been any gains from this tragic event. Had there been a positive side to any of this? No, he told himself, there had been no positive outcome. Why, even the town's tree was a victim, having also been ripped away. Tears filled his eyes as he looked up, up, straining to see all the way to the treetop. It was so big and had been so beautiful. It just wasn't the same anymore. Nothing was the same anymore. Even though the birds and squirrels continued to make their homes in the branches, their nests were exposed, whereas before they had been protected and hidden by the leaves.

Then Tom noticed something—something almost too small to see. *What in the world*, he thought. He got up and walked over to get a closer look. *By golly*, he exclaimed to himself. There were green patches on that tree everywhere! Tiny little buds were forming all over the branches—hundreds of them. Treestone was not dead after all, but was very much alive! For the first time in that long, sad year, Tom's spirit rose within him and he felt a sense of hope.

Quickly he ran off to tell someone—anyone—that the tree was alive! People hurried to the park to see for themselves. Word spread rapidly throughout the town that Treestone was alive, and that night the park was humming with activity. It wasn't as though there was any actual hope was in the tree itself, but rather that the tree represented a hope they felt had been taken away when the accident happened.

Treestone not only lived but thrived. True, it looked somewhat different with its missing limb and split trunk, but nonetheless, it healed and went on to live for many more years. Leaves hid countless bird and squirrel nests; people once again rested and played and talked in its shade; and in wintertime, the hoarfrost continued to bedazzle passers-by with glittering, frozen jewels.

The secret to Treestone's amazing resurrection had taken place deep in the ground where no one could see. Throughout the tree's one hundred-year lifespan, it had endured many dry spells by sending its roots down deep, deep into the soil to find water. Its roots had provided not only water for nourishment but also stability for when the winds came. The hardships of the droughts and winds were what had enabled Treestone to grow into a mighty oak. Its response, to send its roots down deep, was actually the very reason it had survived the trauma.

If a tree's roots are shallow, it will surely topple over in a windstorm or die of thirst, but when the roots are deep, they hold the tree firmly in place when the winds attack, and it never goes without water. How about you? Are your roots deep enough for you to endure a very hard trial?

Application

For those going through hardships and crises

Explanation

God does not give anyone a perfect or easy life after becoming a Christian. If we were to view a graph of a Christian's spiritual walk, we would not see a straight line upward representing spiritual growth; rather, we would see dips and peaks, with the line progressing ever upward in spite of the dips.

We cannot reach spiritual maturity without problems, crises, hardships, or trauma. If that were so, we would become prideful and have no need for God. It is through those trials that we have the <u>opportunity</u> to grow. We don't have to reach out to God, but we certainly can. While we're going through valleys of pain, we are most apt to go to Him and ask for His power to help us. When His Spirit comes into us, our "self" begins to be driven out. As we yield to God's Spirit by spending time with Him every day in prayer, with others in Christian fellowship, and by reading the Bible, we get to know God personally, and our thoughts begin to change to be more Christ-like. Over time, we learn the characteristics of God and we begin to take on those characteristics. That is called transformation, and it happens mostly when we are in our "low" times—our valleys.

As we go through difficult trials and cling to our Heavenly Father in prayer, our roots of faith are growing, going deeper and deeper each day. Growth is often a painful process (thus the term "growing pains") and when the breakthrough comes, we rejoice in what He has done. We breathe easier and relax more, sometimes even to the point that we stop reading the Word and spending time with Him. The next time a trial comes our way, though, we remember to go to Him for strength and encouragement. Again, our roots begin to go deeper as we search for as answers—as we long to be with Him and to fellowship again. It is all a learning process, and the mature Christian is one who sets time apart daily to be with God, not just in times of trouble. Fortunately for us, God loves and takes us as we are.

God is loving and forgiving, and He cares for you more than you could ever imagine. He loves for us to be with Him and to get to know Him, so try to remember to go to Him every day. Ask Him for what you need, and tell Him everything you feel and think. He already knows, but when you let go and trust in Him, He will take you places you never dreamed possible!

Letting go of our problems and giving them to Christ allows us the opportunity to hold on tightly to His hand. (It is very difficult to grab onto something new if you already have a hand full of something else!) Even though you cannot see Him, God is real and He is with you all the time. Never does He follow you around to spy on you, or to scold you for doing wrong. His only desire is to love you and for you to know Him and to love Him. If you cannot do this, tell Him and ask Him to help you love and desire Him. As crazy as that may sound, He will honor your request and draw you even closer!

GIANT TRUCK

You are driving on a two-lane highway behind a giant truck that is going very slowly. You are frustrated because you feel stuck. Other cars are passing both you and the giant truck and although you want to pass, you are intimidated by the truck's size. You think to yourself, "If that huge truck hits me, my car will look like a pancake. What if the wind pushes me off the highway while I'm trying to pass? But I can't stand driving so slowly anymore. I have to try!"

Finally, you decide to give it a try. You press down hard on the gas pedal. As you are passing, however, fear grips you again. "This truck is really huge! Will I be able to make it?" With this doubt in your mind, you unconsciously reduce your speed. Now you're about midway past the truck, but you're not making any headway.

"Should I just slow down and fall behind the truck again?" All of a sudden, you remember how miserable you were behind the truck. You decide again to face your fears and increase your speed. You keep going until you pass the giant truck. A wave of relief sweeps over you, and you feel joyous for having faced your fears and conquering the giant!

APPLICATION

Coping with challenges in your life

EXPLANATION

We all have challenges—"giants"—in our lives. When we have to face one, we have a choice to make: we can decide to give up and feel sorry for ourselves (like a driver stuck behind a truck) or we can decide to do whatever it takes to conquer the giant (like a driver stepping on the gas and making it around the truck). The decision is ours alone to make.

There are many giants that we will face in our lifetime: finding a job, making a marriage work, struggling to complete an important task, facing a controlling co-worker. If you shrink behind your giants and try to hide, you will begin feeling angry, depressed, and bitter. You may start blaming the situation, person, or thing. You may even be angry with God for putting you in such a bad predicament.

Instead of staying in a desperate state of mind, you can choose to face your giants. But be sure of this: facing your giants is never easy. Discouragement may come and try to keep you from fighting the battle.

In the Bible, we read of David and Goliath. David conquered his giant by thinking it was too big to miss rather than too big to hit! David recognized that God was with him.

You will not be able to conquer your giants without God's help. When you do your part by giving it your all, God will do His part by intervening on your behalf in supernatural ways. In other words, when you trust God, He will make up for what you don't have!

If you lose your job, you have to put effort into finding a new one and know that God is in control of the situation. As long as you are doing your part—applying for jobs—God will do His part and find the right job for you at the right moment. If you don't get a job right away and start feeling discouraged, keep on trying and believing that God is in control. You will not see God's blessing unless you keep trying until God shows you His faithfulness.

Challenges/Crises in Life

The Giant of Unemployment

Facing his own giant of unemployment, Henry was impacted by the economic crisis when the company he worked for began to downsize. He, as well as all his co-workers, was afraid of losing his job. The atmosphere had become depressing. It had started slowly—first with his work schedule being reduced from five days a week to four, and then eventually to three. One day, his worst nightmare became reality when his boss called him into the office and told him that he was being laid off. He was to pack up his belongings and go home.

Henry was very depressed. He called his wife and told her about it. He had no idea how to support his family now. He felt like a failure. This was Henry's "giant" and he did not know how to face it and conquer it.

Unemployment checks were not enough to get them through the month, and the bills began to pile up. Although his wife, Jackie, encouraged him to look for work, Henry was sinking into depression and self-pity. He felt like a failure and didn't even want to get up in the mornings and face the new day.

He and Jackie began fighting more and more often, but sometimes he felt too discouraged even to fight. At those times, he would simply sit on the couch and stare at the ceiling.

Then one day as Jackie prepared for her Sunday school class, she read the story about how David defeated the giant, Goliath, with a simple slingshot and five little stones. Suddenly, a light came on in her mind, and she realized that she and Henry were facing a "giant"!

At that very moment, she decided to not let despair overtake her anymore. She got on her knees and prayed for God's help. She had peace and felt Him inspire her to look for work.
She had been a stay-at-home-mom and didn't think she had many job skills, but nonetheless, she was determined to roll up her sleeves and face her giant. She would depend on God like she never had before. Not only did she look on various websites for work but she also walked boldly into stores and restaurants with resume in hand.

Although Jackie felt that she was doing what God wanted her to do, this was by no means a "quick fix." Several months passed with no job offers, but she remained diligent. When she felt hopeless, she would get on her knees again and pray to God. She expressed all her feelings—anxiety, fear, worry—but she knew God was big enough to handle her emotions. After all, hadn't He given feelings to her in the first place? She read the Bible with new fervor, taking in its words of hope and of God's love and mercy. She let the Scriptures minister to her heart and in so doing, became energized to get through the days with peace and joy. In spite of her lack of job experience, Jackie felt confident that the Lord would provide her with work that would supplement their income.

Then one day, she received a call for an interview at a local bank and was hired on the spot. The journey had been difficult; in fact, it felt at times that it had been all uphill. Jackie rejoiced that the Lord had listened to her plea and had rewarded her diligence.

Encouraged by his wife's faith, Henry's faith in God began to grow. His prayer time lengthened, and he began to read the Bible more faithfully. He started learning about God's character and of His love for mankind. Henry began to heal emotionally, and he started applying for various jobs that he had found on the Internet. Knowing Jackie had struggled while she looked for a job helped him do the same. Endurance took root.

The Giant of Troubled Marriage

Jim and Melody were struggling. They'd had four wonderful years of marriage, and even after the birth of their little boy, things were good. They spent a lot of time together playing as a couple and as a family. To each it felt like a fairy tale and they couldn't understand it when others talked of having trouble. Jim and Melody gave each other and their little one undivided attention and looked forward to being together after work every day.

Then one day Jim told Melody that his parents needed his help on their farm. They were getting older and were no longer able to do the chores by themselves, plus they didn't have enough money to pay someone else. Night after night he went there after work, coming home late, dirty, and exhausted. Melody tried to be understanding, but loneliness set in and she felt ignored. Not only that, but there were many projects that needed his attention. Although she tried not to nag, she did, in the hopes of coercing him into "choosing" her again. This had the opposite effect, however, and Jim started feeling closed in, as though he had lost his freedom. He, too, was becoming resentful—not of his parents but of his wife.

Jim was being pulled in two directions. His parents needed him, and he loved them and wanted to help out. His wife also needed him but in a different way, and he loved her, too. It felt like he had to choose. Jim and Melody were facing their giant: a troubled marriage.

They had a choice to make. They could stay in their marriage as it was and wait for it to die, or they could get professional help to face their troubles and save their marriage. Repairing a relationship is never easy. Facing issues is never easy. It is difficult to admit you are wrong, and it is difficult to say, "I'm sorry." For that to happen, it is necessary for individuals to look at themselves and admit their own flaws and weaknesses. It takes courage to be vulnerable, and most people do not want to subject themselves to the scrutiny of someone else.

A good marriage, with closeness and intimacy, consists of vulnerability, transparency, and faithfulness. It is just as important to be honest as it is to keep marriage confidentialities. If you are going to tell your friends the things that your spouse has done wrong, why should he or she open up to you? Talking confidently with a counselor will help heal your emotions, much like lancing a boil of infection will help it heal—from the inside out.

Many times people in a troubled marriage think the best thing to do is to get out and find someone else. Though that may feel good for a while, what really happens is that each person carries old baggage into a new marriage and the same problems, plus brand new ones, come to the surface. It's like buying a new refrigerator and putting in it all the rotten food from your old one. Your new fridge is going to stink to high heaven!

A seventy-year-old grandmother once told her granddaughter, "I have married five times and have divorced five times. I kept carrying the same old problems from one marriage to another. I should have gotten help for my first marriage and worked things out."

If Jim and Melody give up on their marriage now, they would have more problems in all their relationships later on. And most of all, their little boy, who is completely innocent and not understanding, needs both parents in his life. Living in a separate household would not be a good option. All children need their whole family in order to have security. With constant fighting and struggling, children's basic needs are undermined as they fear that their parents will separate or get divorced. One nine-year-old told his school counselor that he was tired at school every day because he couldn't sleep at night until his parents stop fighting. It is a nightmare for children to think that their parents will separate.

If you put God in the center of your relationship, there is hope. God can show each of you what to do to make a positive difference in your relationship. If you learn to love God more than you love your spouse and children, you could be lifted up by God, even when you are alone. No one can give you unconditional love except God. Others, including your spouse and children, can only supply *some* of your needs *some* of the time. Allow God to supply *all* of your needs *all* of the time. Counting on your spouse and others for occasional support is a very realistic expectation.

Facing the Giant of Amnesia

Tony faced an uncertain future. A construction worker with a twenty-eight-year history, he had recently experienced a work-related, closed-head injury that left him with a severe case of amnesia. He had no recollection of his work, his girlfriend, his childhood, family members, his apartment or even his name.

When he first visited Dr. Rita, she observed that he appeared to be scared, sad, and mad all at the same time. How could Tony be expected to face such a horrible giant such as this? Not knowing whether he'd ever work again, he faced the seemingly impossible task of sorting out what was what and who was who, let alone trying to figure out how to pay his bills.

Giving up on life seemed like a good idea to Tony. In the mornings, he stayed in bed with the covers tightly over his head. If the phone rang, he ignored it. If someone came to the door, he ignored that, too. He wished that the earth would open up and swallow him whole. Then one day his pastor contacted Dr. Rita in the hopes that she could help. She agreed and much to the pastor's surprise, Tony came in for the appointment.

At first, Tony seemed apprehensive and said he didn't really care much for therapists as they'd never done him any good. It took a few sessions but slowly Tony began letting down his guard and trusting Dr. Rita.

Dr. Rita told him that she thought he must feel frustrated because no one could help him and that he must worry about whether or not he would get well again. Tears ran down his cheeks when he realized that his feelings were understood. He continued to share what he could remember. As Dr. Rita continued to reflect in a way that had meaning to him, Tony continued to remember bits and pieces of his past. He remembered a woman who had visited him in the hospital who said she was his girlfriend. As her visits continued, and as she continued to love him just the way he was, he began remembering even more about his life.

Even though Tony's memory was improving, he suffered with severe headaches. He also worried a great deal about his mother, his girlfriend, about having a job again—and of his future in general. Facing this giant was taking its toll, but he did not give up. He took up Dr. Rita's suggestion of volunteering at the church and did chores of all types. Once again he was useful and busy, and life was getting better.

One day while working there, he collapsed onto the floor with a severe headache. He was taken to the hospital for observation and treatment. His family and friends worried that he would lose the precious memories he had been regaining. When he didn't show up for his appointment with Dr. Rita, she prayed that God would take care of him and perform a healing miracle in his life.

Two weeks later in her office, Tony told Dr. Rita his amazing story. Not only could he still recall what previously had been lost, but he remembered even more. He remembered happenings of his long-ago childhood, of his parents, his family, and his job and how the accident had happened.

After much counseling and prayer, Tony was able to go back to work and retrain. At first it was part-time and then full-time. Everyone rejoiced with him and called him a walking miracle!

In Toni's case, he had a pastor, a family, friends, a girlfriend, and a counselor who would not give up on him. Instead, they all encouraged him with words, actions, and prayer to get him through the tough times. It was these combined efforts that gave him the strength and persistence to face his giant. His faith grew; his abilities returned. God filled in where Tony lacked. That's how God works. One minute at a time, an hour at a time, a day at a time, little by little, step by step.

Are You Ready to Face Your Giant?

Are you facing a giant in your life? Do you feel like giving up? God loves you so much that He will never let go of you. And He wants you to reach out and take hold of His hand. He is bigger than any giant you will ever have. In fact, He could hold the giant in his hand and crush it. Do you have faith that God would win the battle for you? Fighting your giant alone would be frightening because you never know for sure whether or not you can conquer it.

"And we know in all things God works for the good of those who love him, who have been called according to his purpose" (Romans 8:28). God exercises His power when you are totally surrendered to Him. When you still hold on to what you want, God cannot help you. First, He wants you to let go of everything.

Let go and let God!

We all have giants in our lives. It is our choice to defeat them or let them conquer us. If you choose to let your giants defeat you, you will end up stuck in an emotional dungeon. But if you choose to fight your fears and face your giants, God will be there to help you. Just do your best and God will do the rest.

With His help, you can become "more than a conqueror through Him who loves us (Romans 8:37).

THE LITTLE SPARROW

Silence shrouds the tropical forest. Everything seems to have stopped. The birds have hushed their singing; the monkeys, their chattering, and even the insects have ceased their buzzing. The darkened sky sends townsfolk scurrying away to their dwellings where they find refuge and safety.

A storm is quickly approaching the forest!

The wind picks up, sending leaves helter-skelter, and tree branches moan as they sway back and forth. Thunder rolls in the distance and huge raindrops crash through the trees and onto the ground. It begins pouring, and lightning scoots across the sky. The silence has been chased away by the deafening thunder, wind, and rain.

In the middle of the forest, a huge oak tree stands with its mighty limbs spread out wide. On one sits a little sparrow, protected from the storm by a single large leaf.

In the midst of the gale, this little bird has found shelter under the shadow of a leaf.

The clapping thunder, flashing lighting, and pounding rain do not bother this little sparrow for he knows that God is watching over him. No matter how horrible the storm, he is under God's care. He has total confidence that He will stop the storm eventually and the sky will turn blue once again; then he will be able to fly away and continue exploring nature.

Once the storm passes and the sparrow flies, he sees a robin who asks, "Why do these anxious human beings rush about and worry so?"

The sparrow replies, "I think they don't have a Heavenly Father who cares for them like you and me" (Elizabeth Cheney).

APPLICATION

Faith in God / God's love

EXPLANATION

Nowhere in the Bible does God ever say that the Christian walk will be an easy one. He does, however, promise to carry us through each storm that comes our way. When we face any type of difficulty, it is easy to try and fix our problems ourselves, using the limited knowledge and understanding that we possess. But when that doesn't work and we get stuck, we find ourselves running to God, desperately asking for His help. When we have finished praying, we begin to doubt that God will truly handle the situation, and we pick up our burden and carry it right back home again!

This is much like Don, who had a chair that needed to be repaired. Few others appreciated the chair, but to him it was extremely valuable. He had done his best to fix it, but to no avail. One day Don decided to render the services of a reputable woodworker. The merchant assured him that yes, he knows just what to do and will call when it is ready to be picked up. Don left a deposit, the two men shook hands, and Don headed back to the truck. Halfway there, however, he had a little nagging doubt that the woodworker would fix the chair, so he turned around, got his chair, put it in the truck, and took it home. The woodworker simply stared in disbelief, still holding the deposit in his hand.

When we have a need that we cannot handle, we go to God and ask Him to help. Knowing exactly what to do with the situation, He reaches out and takes the burden from us. Relieved, we continue on with our day, free from the stress of wondering what on earth we should do to remedy our problem. Pretty soon, however, we think of several ways that the problem could be fixed, and we begin to meddle. Before long, we are carrying the burden again and God is standing back, all the while watching us and sorrowfully wishing we would put all our trust in Him.

Our Lord longs for us to be more like the little sparrow who knows his Heavenly father is with him throughout the storm. Instead of being afraid, he rests in God's arms and allows Him to provide the shelter in the storm. Sparrow has total trust that God will calm the storm and bring back a sunny sky. He knows God is in control.

Are you like the little sparrow?

Desi learned to be trusting, like the sparrow, after a period of struggles on her own. Once in the wee hours of the morning, her husband, Mark, woke up, disoriented and unable to talk. Desi called an ambulance and Mark was soon whisked away to the hospital where doctors tried without success to find what was wrong with him. Test after test was done, but no diagnosis was found.

In the meantime, Desi was trying to keep the family together, going back and forth to the hospital, caring for the children and keeping up with the bills and paperwork. She was both afraid of the future and in denial that this could be happening. When the doctors told her that Mark may not recover, she felt hopeless. Money was running out, the house was turned upside down, the car needed repairs, and she was sick and tired of it all.

At night, she dragged herself to bed and then was unable to sleep. She began coughing frequently and pain wracked her body. She wondered what her life was going to be like with two young children to care for and no income or help from Mark. Her fear turned to anger. Her prayers didn't seem to help because she was so desperate for immediate relief.

Fortunately, friends and relatives gave her lots of emotional and physical support, which was very comforting to her, but nonetheless, she still could not experience the peace that she used to have with God.

She wasn't even sure if He was going to help her husband. Her faith was shaken.

Then one night, she was in so much emotional turmoil that she realized she simply could not handle the situation by herself anymore. She knew she was unable, but deep in her heart, she knew God was fully able. She did not understand, but God did. She was weak, but God was strong. There was nothing left to do but to give it all entirely to God. If she didn't, she knew she would probably have an emotional breakdown and maybe lose everything.

That night, she prayed and turned it all over to Him. Mark's healing, the finances, the dirty house and car repairs, she gave it all. A sense of peace came quietly over her. She was able to be like the little sparrow that trusts God in the middle of the storm. At night, she began imagining herself wrapped in her heavenly Father's loving arm and gently being rocked to sleep. When she visited Mark at the hospital, she told herself that God was her husband's Healer and whatever negative messages she got from the doctors would not matter. God is the Master Physician and He knows exactly what to do!

After surrendering it all to God, she was able to see God's healing hand in her husband's body. He was regaining his strength; his speech began to return, and all without a diagnosis. From this experience, she learned to be like the little sparrow resting in her heavenly Father's arms in the middle of the storm.

"He will take delight in her, he will quiet her with his love, and He will rejoice over her with singing" (Zephaniah 3: 17).

The old hymn, "His Eye Is on the Sparrow,"* came to Desi's mind. In part it says, "Why should I feel discouraged? Why should the shadows come? Why should my heart be lonely and long for heaven and home? His eye is on the sparrow and I know He watches me. I sing because I'm happy. I sing because I'm free. For His eye is on the sparrow and I know He watches me!"

---

* Martin, Civilla D. "His Eye Is on the Sparrow." 1905.

CHALLENGES/CRISES IN LIFE

SMALL VOICE IN A NOISY ROOM

It was Saturday night and Larry and Liz were hosting a party. The house was full of people, and it was very noisy. The dog barked when the doorbell rang, unruly children ran around the dining room table "shooting" each other as they played cowboys and Indians, and the television was blaring in the living room. In order to be heard, everyone had to shout. The constant noise made everything chaotic and unenjoyable.

There's an old saying that opposites attract, and it was true in this case. Larry was a big man who carried himself well, had a deep voice and keen ears, and was a successful salesman. On the other hand, Liz was small in stature, enjoyed staying home and caring for her family, and had a rather soft voice.

At one point during the party, Liz needed to talk to Larry, so she whispered in his ear. He was busy as usual dominating a conversation, and stopping to listen to her was the last thing he wanted to do . . . so he simply ignored her.

Liz was hurt and angry at her husband's rudeness. As she sulked and felt sorry for herself, she decided to teach him a lesson and give him the silent treatment for the rest of the night. Larry, however, was so busy with all the attention that he didn't even notice what Liz was doing.

APPLICATION

Relationship with God

EXPLANATION

Sometimes your brain is noisy, just like the loud party at Larry and Liz's. Thoughts come at you fast, such as what you are going to do next, how to deal with a certain individual, a problem that needs to be solved, or an unpleasant conversation you had earlier. Every once in a while, your brain gets overloaded and is unable to tune out the input it's been getting all day long.

Did it ever occur to you that God may be whispering to you about something He wants you to hear? He has words that can calm you down and give you insight. But if you are so busy talking to yourself that God cannot get your attention, you will miss out on the blessing He has for you. God is very patient and will wait until you are ready to stop and listen to Him. In the meantime, it makes Him sad to see you struggle unnecessarily when you could feel so much better by quieting your mind and letting go. Is God waiting for you to make time for Him? When are you going to stop struggling and start listening?

Larry's life was like that. As soon as he arose in the morning, he turned on the radio to hear the news and then went about his ritual of getting ready for work. In the process he had no time to listen to Liz or his kids, four-year-old Stevie and two-year-old Matt.

The chaos continued on his drive to work. With the volume of the car radio cranked up, he couldn't even hear his own thoughts. When he arrived at work, things got even crazier. As a salesman, it was his job to persuade people to buy from him and he took no thought in stealing customers from fellow salespeople. His physique attracted people to him, his strong voice kept their attention, and his knowledge of the products was convincing to buyers.

But poor Larry was unaware of his huge problem. He did not know that his co-workers and his family were tired of his self-righteous and egotistical attitude. His business and financial success had caused him to wrongly believe that he was successful in all areas of his life.

One day it dawned on him that his sales were down. At first, he blamed the sour economy, but even then he realized that return customers were not coming back to see him; rather, they were seeking out other salesmen. After two months of losing repeat business, he became angry—angry at everyone but himself. He blamed his co-workers for stealing customers; he blamed Liz for keeping him awake at night, and he blamed the kids for being too noisy. All the while, he never looked at his own behavior or what he might do to make things better.

Larry could not fathom what in the world was going wrong. Things at home and work were the way they always had been, but something was different now and he couldn't figure it out. In his drives to and from work, he thought about the developing problems. Even though he found it distracting to think hard with the radio blasting, it didn't occur to him to turn it off and try to make some peace. He had always done best with chaos, he reasoned, and couldn't possibly make sense of anything if it was quiet.

Money problems made things worse at home. He and Liz fought more often and with greater intensity. The boys reacted negatively to the stress by demanding attention from their dad. Liz became emotionally drained and suggested they try counseling. At that, Larry blew up, angry that she thought they had a problem and dead-set against talking to some stranger about their lives.

It became clear to Liz that nothing was going to change between her and Larry, and one day she packed up the kids and the car and went to stay with her mother several hours away. When Larry came home from work that night, instead of finding the usual noise, chaos, and upset, he found a cold, empty house. The note lying on the table summed it up. It was over, Liz had written, and he could live life his own way. She and the boys were moving on.

The impact was immediate, and Larry fell to his knees. For the first time in his life, he cried out to God from his heart. His sobs came from deep within, and tears fell like rain. He had no idea at all what to do. Throughout the evening and all through the night, his sobs continued. Liz would not answer his calls, and questions kept coming at him. Sleep eluded him that night, and by morning he was drained. He called in sick for the first time ever, and stayed home to try and make sense of the mess.

The house was silent. No kids. No wife. No radio. No TV. Nothing to distract him. Around lunchtime, he sat on the couch and opened a Bible. He realized he hadn't read it in years, and reasoned as to why God would even help him now, after neglecting Him for so long. But as he read, a peace began to settle in his heart. That night Larry slept peacefully for a little while, and went to work the next day. There was lots of confusion in his mind, and his sales were still down, but he kept thinking about that peace he'd experienced the day before; it was different, and he wanted more of it. That night at home, he again picked up the Bible and read. He talked to God and hoped to hear His voice. Television remained turned off, and while the silence was unusual to him, it was also somehow pleasant. As time passed, the quietness became a refuge, and Larry's time spent with God began to bear fruit. He started understanding his own flaws and shortcomings and knew that God was healing him from the inside out.

A month went by, then two, then three. Divorce papers were served, and Larry was ordered to pay both wife and child support. His paychecks dwindled to a third of what he'd been bringing home, and financially, it was horrible for him. Visiting the kids every other weekend was brutal as well, not only because it was hard to keep up with their lives, but because the drive back and forth was tiresome. Nonetheless, Larry was determined, no matter what, to put God first and learn to rely on Him to make the best of this bad situation.

Time spent with God is always for the best. Larry began to see how detrimental the chaos had been. Slowly he resolved to have a peaceful life and honest relationships. Co-workers saw this change almost immediately, as Larry had been such a brute, and at first they didn't know how to respond. Eventually they began to trust that maybe he was really being honest, and as the trust grew, the relationships became stronger. Larry no longer tried to take business away from other salesmen, and he no longer tried to talk customers into sales. Instead, he was more focused on staying true to God and working within the clients' financial means. People began to respect him as they never had before.

Over the course of a year, Larry turned his entire life over to God, as often happens once a person has lost everything. He became involved at church, joined a men's Bible study, and continued to make daily Bible reading and quiet time with God a priority. His spirit was now calm and he was peaceful, and he could more clearly understand and discern truth through God's words as he read scripture.

Larry continued adjusting to being alone, and hated with all his heart that his family had broken up. He came to understand, however, the role he had had in it and was willing to accept every aspect of his personal responsibility.

One day the phone rang, and it was Liz. He hardly recognized her voice through the sobbing and weeping, and he wondered what on earth had happened. After a few minutes, she was able to pour her heart out to him, telling him she missed him and what they had once had together. The children missed their daddy. Nothing was right. In fact, everything was wrong.

They agreed to meet at a midway restaurant to talk things over. This would be the first time in over a year that they had even seen each other. With much anticipation, they met and confessed their wrongdoings and asked each other for forgiveness. At the end of the conversation, Larry asked her to go out with him again, and Liz accepted his invitation. They dated for a while: sometimes the children would come along. Gradually the family began to heal, and they finally moved back in together.

Larry and Liz both knew and understood that in order to continue healing, they each had to give God top priority every day. They found peace in the scriptures and in their respective quiet times and they often shared with each other what they had learned that day.

The chaos that once controlled their lives gave way to peace and order, which was reflected most apparently through the children's good behavior.

Proverbs 21:21 says, "He who pursues righteousness and love finds life, prosperity, and honor." Tune out those random thoughts that race through your brain; and tune in to the voice of God! You will live a better life. It is never too late to have a second chance!

CHRISTIAN LIVING

BIKE RIDING WITHOUT THE TRAINING WHEELS

Sara, five years old, had been riding her bicycle, with training wheels attached, to keep from falling to the ground. She liked to feel the breeze on her face and the freedom of riding on her own. One day Sara's father took the training wheels off so she could learn to ride without assistance. At first, she was nervous but when she realized that her daddy would be there to hold on and to catch her if she fell, she felt safe again. She totally trusted her father.

Sara's dad held onto the bike until he was certain she could balance herself, and then he let go. For the first time, she was on her own! She kept her balance for a little while and then went tumbling to the ground. Her daddy came right over to help her up and to brush off the dirt. Although she had skinned her knee, Sara realized that she was okay. She smiled because her father had watched over and made sure she was all right, even when she fell. As long as she trusted his guidance, she would be okay.

Time and time again, Sara's daddy was there to guide her and offer encouragement. Her confidence grew, and soon she was able to ride all by herself.

Sara became an expert bicyclist and continued riding into adulthood. Although it was highly uncommon, she did have a mishap once, and it landed her in the doctor's office with a broken arm, but her initiative to find help healed her wounds so that she could ride her bike again.

APPLICATION

Faith in God / God's love

EXPLANATION

The Christian life is a journey, and on it you will experience many struggles. If you focus on your own circumstances rather than having total reliance on God, you will feel discouraged and afraid and experience a loss of balance.

Your heavenly Father will help and comfort you because you are precious and honored in His sight and because He loves you (Isaiah 43:4). He will speak to you and encourage you through His words.

"Do not be afraid, for I am with you. Do not be dismayed, for I am your God. I will strengthen you. I will help you. I will uphold you with my victorious right hand" (Isaiah 41:10).

With God's encouragement, you will be able to get up and try again. He has not promised an easy life after you become a Christian, but He does promise to be there with you when you go through difficulties. The sky is not always blue, but when it turns dark, you can have faith that God will turn the sky blue again. When you have full reliance on God, your fear will be lessened. Trust conquers fear.

Sara had total reliance on her earthly father because she trusted his protection and guidance. When her fear dissipated, she was able to stay balanced on her bike without the training wheels.

As you mature in your Christian walk, you still will fall at times. Depending on your own wisdom to deal with life's struggles can cause you to fall away from God, making you stressed, overwhelmed, and heavily burdened. Once you decide to give up the control and let God take over, you will see Him at work in your circumstances. He can orchestrate the situation and heal your wounds, just like the doctor who healed Sara's arm when she fell off her bike as an adult. Sara had to make a doctor appointment so her wound could be properly treated. In the same way, you must take the initiative to ask God for help.

His personal phone number is Jeremiah 33:3, which states, "Call unto me and I will answer you and tell you great and unsearchable things you do not know." If you are willing to go to God, He will lift you up when situations push you down. Let Him raise you up; let Him pull you in when you are drifting out on your own.

Feed your faith, and your doubt will starve to death.

A Real-Life Story

When Teresa turned sixteen, she attended a Christian camp and there accepted Christ as her personal Savior. She had never experienced such joy and peace as she did after making that life-changing decision. Her heart was so fired up for God that she wanted to share her faith with everyone around. She involved herself with ministries and spent time with her new Christian friends. When she was sad or afraid, she would pray to God and she felt better. When she read the Bible, the words were alive. She was so in love with God that she knew He would be there for her whenever she needed Him.

Back at school, a popular boy named Peter caught Teresa's eye. Not only was he the school's star basketball player but he was also very handsome and charming, and girls flocked around him vying for his attention.

One day out of the blue, Peter called Teresa and asked her out. They had a good time and before long they were spending every waking moment together. At school Peter talked to her exclusively. Her heart fluttered with his pursuit and she began to fall in love.

During this time, God became less important to Teresa as she gave first place to Peter. In fact, Peter became almost like a god to her.

Without realizing it, she was falling further and further away from God. She stopped attending youth group, reading the Bible, and praying. She changed her schedule to accommodate Peter's; she allowed him to take control of her life, and she waited anxiously every day for his phone calls and visits.

It seemed that Peter felt the same way towards Teresa, but truthfully he did not. He was busy with basketball practice, studies, and own social life, and he would sometimes totally forget to call. Plus, he was thoroughly enjoying the attention of the other pretty girls at school.

Teresa became distraught and understood that Peter was not feeling towards her the way she was feeling towards him. She then made the terrible mistake of thinking that if she gave her body to him sexually, she would be able to capture his heart. Soon they were sexually active and any love Peter may have felt turned to lust, and he used her for his own sexual gratification.

During these trying times, Teresa never asked God for help because she knew He probably did not approve of what was happening. The Holy Spirit seemed to tug at her heart, and she secretly knew she should get out of that relationship. However, she was too "in love" to give him up and, at least temporarily, she ended up trading him for God.

The more she pursued Peter, the more he wanted to get away from her, except when he wanted sex, and then he was as sweet as pie. Eventually, however, the phone calls became fewer and further in between. Her world spun out of control and took her even further away from a relationship with God.

Teresa would sit in her room and cry; she missed him so. Her friend, Rebecca, told her that Peter had secretly been dating another girl.

"You need to give him up," Rebecca warned.

Devastated, Teresa fell into a deep depression. She cried night and day, refused to eat, and was unable to sleep. Then, worst of all, she found out that she was pregnant. Peter angrily rejected any responsibility and left Teresa to face her predicament alone.

Then one day while she was in the midst of this painful suffering, she remembered hearing the story about little Sara who had cried out to her father when she fell from her bike.

Immediately Teresa fell to her knees and cried to God, asking him to forgive her sins and restore her to Him. Right then and there, God gave her a peace that was beyond understanding. With her renewed strength through Christ, her parent's support and understanding, and her

Christian friends' love, Teresa made the heart-wrenching decision to carry the baby to full term and then give it up for adoption. She knew she was totally unprepared to raise a child, and this was the only way to give it a high quality of life.

God's love towards Teresa remained throughout this heart- and gut-wrenching ordeal. When she turned back to God, He immediately embraced her and held her tightly. His unconditional love, and the encouragement she received from the Holy Spirit, sustained and strengthened her, allowing her to deal with what seemed to be an impossible situation.

"With God all things are possible" (Matthew 19:26). His love will never fail you.

BOOMERANG

It was a sunny fall day and young college students were having fun throwing their boomerangs in a large, grassy field. When you throw a football, soccer ball, baseball, Frisbee, or paper airplane into the air, it will fly up and then land on the ground. Boomerangs are different in that when they are thrown, they fly in an oblong angle and return. Someone skilled in throwing boomerangs can actually stand in the same spot and catch it on its return. Thrown correctly, boomerangs will not fall to the ground as other objects do; they always come back.

APPLICATION

Blaming

EXPLANATION

Some people like to blame others for their own hurt. As stated in the Bible, There is a time when a man lords it over others to his own hurt

(Ecclesiastes 8:9). Blaming others takes the responsibility for your own feelings and mistakes and puts it on someone else. This may give the blamer a false sense of superiority, or it can give him an excuse to not make decisions for himself and simply stay in a wait-and-see mode.

When you think you have no need of taking responsibility for yourself, you begin to think your life, your feelings, your thoughts, and your circumstances are entirely someone else's fault. This creates drama, which may get some of your friends to have sympathy for you, but you may eventually find yourself tossing and turning in bed every night because your life is so miserable.

When you make others responsible for your hurt, it is like throwing a boomerang—the hurt and consequences always come right back to you.

The blame game has many disadvantages. For example, as long as you blame others for your misfortune, you cannot experience joy because you will be holding on to hurt and anger. By disempowering yourself, you will stop making good decisions, and you could actually become stuck in life through self-pity. You will become a victim of the circumstances you yourself create. Blaming someone else actually gives that person power over you.

This is a very dangerous emotional game of control because, in reality, you are manipulating others so they will do for you what you do not want to do for yourself. By blaming someone else, you talk yourself out of making healthy—and sometimes difficult—decisions.

Having some kind of control is one of our basic human needs. When you feel like you are not in control of your situation, you feel bad about yourself. When you are so focused on the hurt, you are unable to appreciate what you do have. Being stuck emotionally also stunts your spiritual growth. When you're very hurt, there is no room for God, but without God's help, you will have a hard time letting go of the hurt.

Others may hurt you, but it is up to you to decide what to do with the hurt. You can hold on to it forever, blame someone else, and lock yourself into an emotional dungeon. You may think by doing so that you are putting someone else in a prison, but you end up finding yourself a prisoner instead. It is like when you throw the boomerang in the air; it comes back to you. Do you want to be forever a victim or do you want to be a victor where you can do something about it to get yourself out of your self-made prison?

Here is an example of a woman, Julia, who was brought up in an abusive home. When she became an adult, she married Tom, an alcoholic. The couple gets into fights every time Julia complains about his drinking problem. She urges him to get help, but he does not think he has a problem, and then Julia feels helpless. As long as Julia keeps thinking that her husband is responsible for her happiness, she is stuck. One day she realized she needed help, and she sought the advice of a counselor.

The counselor, Dr. Rita, told her the story of the boomerang, and Julia recognized she was responsible for her own happiness. Instead of blaming Tom, she decided to get help to deal with the situation. She remembered Dr. Rita telling her to focus on herself and the decisions she could make. She had no control over Tom's problem, but she did have control of her own life. She enrolled in school so she could someday have a career, and she excelled in her classes. She joined a support group with women of alcoholic spouses and learned that she was not alone in dealing with those particular issues. She decided to take piano lessons. She continued counseling to work on her own issues, and most importantly, she prayed to God every day.

God began changing Julia's heart and filling it with love, and as a result she discovered that other things became less important to her. When she felt sad, she cried out to God for comfort. When she felt happy, she thanked Him for the blessings. At all times she could play to her heart's content on the piano, putting music to her emotions.

As long as she focused on God and made the best of her circumstances, she felt her life was under her control. She made a conscious decision to live a victoriously rather than being a victim to her husband.

It amazed her to one day discover that by focusing intently on living a godly life according to the Scriptures, and by not making her husband responsible for her happiness, she began to see a change in

Tom. He used to play the blame game, too, and tried to excuse his abusive behavior by saying it was her fault because she nagged so much. As Julia loved him more and more, without asking him to change, and as she grew content with her life, Tom began to change also. He liked this "new" wife, the one who didn't nag or correct him or throw fits.

He decided to check into rehab to deal with his drinking problem, and although it was a long haul, Tom and Julia slowly grew closer together and began talking about their problems instead of yelling, and asking forgiveness of each other instead of blaming.

Do you find yourself blaming someone else for the circumstances in your life? If so, you may want to seek help in stopping the vicious cycle. Once you find that you can have control for yourself, you will find new freedom to grow, to love, to give, and to heal. Your life will never be the same again.

ERASABLE CARDBOARD PAD

Do you remember the erasable cardboard pad you can get in the dollar store? There is a plastic film on top with a little plastic pen attached to it. Using the plastic pen, you can write or draw things on the plastic cover. When you open the plastic cover, everything you have created on the board disappeared. It is a blank page again for you to write or draw on it.

APPLICATION
Dealing with sin and forgiveness

EXPLANATION
Larry used to lie, steal, and abuse alcohol. He hid wine bottles all over the house. When his wife would ask him whether he had been

drinking, he would lie to her. Larry worked in a grocery store where he had access to alcohol. When he did not have extra money to buy alcohol, he would take money from his son's account to buy it. One time he was stopped by the police and was put in jail when he failed the Breathalyzer. While he was in jail, he gave his life to God. He wrote all of his past sins on one of those erasable pads and asked for God's forgiveness. After he prayed, he opened the plastic film of the pad, and everything he had written on it disappeared completely. In the same way that his words disappeared from that pad, his sins were forgiven; God had erased them all. Neither God nor he could now see anything from Larry's past.

Whether your sin is big or small, when you confess your sin to God, he erases your flaws. Everything in the past vanishes. You start a new page of your life with God. It does not mean that once you accept Christ, you become a saint and will never make mistakes. But you can be assured that every time you go to him and confess your mistakes with a sincere heart, God would forgive and erase your sins because He is a compassionate and forgiving God!

You also need to write down everything you have done wrong to others on an erasable pad and asked them for forgiveness. After you clear the air with them, you can then open the plastic film and erase everything on the pad. Now you can have a clear conscience with God and with those whom you have hurt. When you do that, you will feel so much freedom. You will sleep soundly at night because your stress level will have decreased tremendously. People will see joy on your face again.

FARMER JACK

Young Farmer Jack was sitting on his front porch one day looking out at his crops and feeling quite distressed. In spite of his careful soil preparation, sowing of seeds, and watering of the fields, he was not able to get a good harvest. He sat there for several days, feeling sorry for himself and wondering what to do.

Then he had an idea! He would go to town and buy a healthy cow to help with many of the farming chores. In those days, there were no machines and farmers had to rely on cows and horses to help with the heavy work. As he walked along the pathway towards town, he prayed and asked God to help him choose a cow that would be sufficient for his needs.

Once in town, he found and purchased the perfect cow. Because he had prayed and asked God for help in choosing just the right animal, farmer Jack received lots of blessings, including a great harvest. The animal had provided the help he needed in getting everything done. Every evening when he looked out at the fields, he couldn't help but thank God repeatedly for giving him such prosperity—and such a good cow. Farmer Jack went on to become a very prosperous farmer and was able to afford the finer things in life.

He should have been on top of the world, but he realized that he was, again, very unhappy. He had no one with whom to share his life and possessions. He became a successful but lonely man.

Then he had another idea! Going to town and buying a new cow had worked out so well for him; this time he would go to town and look for a wife. On his way to town, a woman saw him and walked towards him. They began talking to each other and quickly became friends. Jack was so lonely that he wasted no time in pursuing her, and within a few weeks, he had asked her to marry him.

You would think that Farmer Jack would be very happy now because he had a successful farm and a wife with whom to share everything. On the contrary, he was now sadder than ever because no matter what he did, he could not get along with his wife. They quarreled almost daily. He was deeply depressed.

Why do you think God blessed Jack when he bought a cow but did not bless him when he got a wife?

APPLICATION

Christian living

EXPLANATION

Farmer Jack was depressed about his poor harvest and asked God to help him choose the right cow to buy. God honored his request and gave him the best one he had ever owned. Because he sought God first, God gave him the best. But when Farmer Jack was sorrowful and lonely for not having anyone with whom to share his life, he desperately took the situation into his own hands. Thinking that a wife would take care of his problem, he pursued the first woman who came along, without seeking God's guidance in prayer. And thus, his marriage was not blessed by God.

How many of us are like Farmer Jack? We take things into our own hands rather than giving them to God. Too often when we're stuck, we try to fix the problem first, and then pray afterwards. We will receive more blessing when we seek God first.

A Real-Life Story

This is a true story about a young couple who wanted to buy a new car. They had visited several dealers, looking for just the right one. One day, they saw the perfect car on display in the showroom. It was a beautiful gold tone with a white top. They admired the beauty of this car and let the salesperson talk them into buying it.

This was the first car this couple had ever been able to afford, and they treasured it dearly, just as they would take care of a new baby. They cleaned it, shined it, and gave it plenty of tender loving care. Since they did not have children, the car indeed was their baby.

Unfortunately, however, this car gave them a world of trouble. It was worse than any used car they'd ever owned. It was not dependable, and every once in a while, for no apparent reason, it would simply stop running. The couple learned a valuable lesson from this experience.

Instead of asking God for help before they made a purchase, they had taken matters into their own hands and bought the first car that caught their eye.

As the years went by, the family grew, and when it was time to buy a mini-van, they knew just what to do. They prayed before they ever went out and looked for a vehicle. Then the husband saw a newspaper ad for a used mini-van for $15,000. They talked with the owner about the van and the price and explained that they could not afford to pay that much. They could, however, afford to pay $7,000. But the owner was not willing to come down on the price.

Disappointed, the couple prayed together again and were able to "let go" of the van. They continued looking, but it seemed that every vehicle was outside of their price range. They sometimes wondered if their budget would ever allow them to afford one. Nonetheless, they continued to give the matter to God and trust Him for the outcome.

Two weeks later, the owner of the mini-van called and said he had decided to sell the van to them for $7,000 because he and his wife really liked them and wanted them to have it. They said they really wanted their van to go to a good home and were certain that this couple would take good care of it.

They couple was in awe of what God had done! The van proved to be a wonderful investment and lasted for years, taking the family on many trips. Eventually, it was given to their college-aged son when he needed it for transportation. He took friends and young people to Christian fellowship and to church. That van became a blessing to many!

"Seek first the Kingdom of God and His righteousness, and all these things shall be added to you" (Matthew 6:33).

CHRISTIAN LIVING

THE HEADLIGHT

At long last, the big day finally arrived when Rita walked out of the Secretary of State's office with her brand new driver's license. How exciting! She hopped into the car, headed for the freeway and eased into the lane without incident -- she was free as a bee and off to visit friends in a nearby town. Once there, they all had a wonderful time chatting, eating desserts and sharing stories. The time passed quickly and without the girls even noticing, nighttime had arrived. It was time for Rita to go home.

With hugs and well-wishes, Rita got into her car, backed out of the driveway and once again headed for the freeway. About a mile or so down the road, however, she became unsure of the surroundings and realized that she didn't know exactly where she was. Always before she had made this trip during daytime hours when it was light and everything could be clearly seen. Even this morning she could have sworn to know the way like the back of her hand.

But the darkness changed everything and this was not the same at all. Now, dark shadows danced in the moonlight and made it all kind of spooky. Mailboxes resembled people alongside the road, raccoons and opossums scurried off the road as her car approached, and landmarks were either not visible or not recognizable in the dark.

A panicky feeling set in and doubts crowded her thoughts. This was before cell phones or GPSs were invented and Rita had no way to contact someone if she became lost. She could clearly see only see what was directly in front of the car where the headlights shone. She couldn't remember where the intersecting roads were that she needed to take or whether she should turn right or left.

Rita had thoughts of taking a wrong turn and ending up who knew where, or of not seeing a curve in time and going off the road and into a ditch where she could be stranded.

As she continued down the road, she heard a little voice inside her say, "This is your life, Rita. I have planned your entire life this way so that you will have to trust me and rely on me totally." The Lord continued to impress on her to stay faithful in doing whatever He put in front of her. Just as the headlights now clearly lit the way directly in front of her, she was to let God guide her a little at a time throughout her life. "When it's time to do something different, I'll let you know," God seemed to tell her.

APPLICATION

Christian walk or worries about the future

EXPLANATION

God had guided Rita's life since she was born. When it was time for Rita to begin attending school, the only one with availability was a Christian school, so that's where her parents enrolled her. They were not Christian, however, and it was not their intention that she convert to that faith; it was their only alternative.

It was through the teachings in that school that Rita learned about God. When attending a youth Christian retreat as a teenager, she accepted Christ as her personal savior.

Meanwhile, opposition was heavy at home. As her family members were not of the Christian faith, she was often teased and sometimes even the adults would taunt her and label her as the family's "holy cow."

As the years passed, Rita continued to trust God and patiently endured the ridicule. Changes began to take place in her family. In secret, her mother, her sisters and brothers, other family members, and close friends would individually come to her and share stories of heartache or trial and ask if she would pray to her God for help on their behalf. Rita began to have a warm heart for hurting and lonely people everywhere. Her grandfather once said to her, "I have never seen a little girl with so much patience and love for people. Someday, you will be able to help many others."

Years earlier, when Rita had given her life to God, she had no idea that the day would come when members of her own family would receive Christ. God had not revealed that to her.

After graduation, Rita applied to graduate school in the United States with the intention of earning a degree in educational administration. When the university received her file, however, it was mistakenly sent to the wrong department. When Rita arrived on campus for registration, she discovered that she was enrolled in the curriculum for counseling.

Rita was not only shocked; she was also disheartened and extremely discouraged, almost to the point of devastation. But with little time to dally, she opted to continue in that curriculum, at least for the time being, and not try to change her major. She attended the classes and, much to her surprise, discovered that she was very happy in them and stuck it out all the way to the end.

Rita did not understand that the Lord was behind the scenes directing the path He wanted her to take. What she thought were setbacks were really His guiding hand moving circumstances in such a way as to put her where He needed her to be.

After completing her education, she moved to New York City and found work with an insurance company and lodging in an apartment in Manhattan. There she met people from all walks of life and all nationalities. Not only did she struggle with the idea that she had not gotten a job in the field of counseling; she was stressed out because she wasn't making enough money.

Still, however, she continued to trust that God was working things out, but God only let her see what was directly in front of her at any given moment.

At the apartment, Rita had ample occasions to "work" for free, offering professional guidance to people who told her their troubles. She didn't realize that these were precious, golden opportunities directly from God, preparing her even more for the future she would have in counseling.

Eventually, Rita married and had children. After obtaining her Ph.D. in Michigan, she decided to stay home with her children and do volunteer counseling at her church. It was in those "quiet years," as she spent many hours each day with the Lord, that God richly deepened her faith. He showed her how to be a good wife and an effective and loving parent. Again, it was in doing work as a lay counselor that God had equipped her to work with people of all ages and from all walks of life.

With only volunteer work under her belt, she realized it would be almost impossible to find a paying job in the counseling field. She also thought she would need to go back to be licensed to practice.

As always, God was behind the scenes, paving the way for her.

Much to her delight, Rita found that she need not go back to school for her license after all. The situation was complex, and available only for a limited time, but Rita's circumstances miraculously satisfied every requirement. She realized that God blesses her continually, even in circumstances she doesn't know exist. She was ecstatic!

Rita went on to become the director and counselor in a counseling ministry at a local church, where she learned how to be part of the ministry staff, counselor, and administrator. All of this was, again, prepared her to take the next step on the path in which God was leading.

Today, Rita has her own private practice, working with people from all walks of life, nationalities, and ages. She has even had the privilege of counseling pastoral and ministerial staff. When she looks back over the circumstances of her life, she can see how God guided her every step of the way.

She knows now that as God was preparing her, He could not reveal the next step to her; that was where her faith in Him had to grow. God wanted her to trust Him in each step.

When your plans hit a wall, keep in mind that it may be God's way of getting you in line with what He wants you to do! Be in prayer continually, and trust Him always that He will make your paths straight. Sometimes U-turns in life can be a blessing in disguise.

"I am the Lord your God, who teaches you what is best for you, who directs you in the way you should go" (Isaiah 48:17-19).

"Submit to God and be at peace with Him. In His way, prosperity will come to you" (Job 22:21-23).

CHRISTIAN LIVING

PASS THE MESSAGE GAME

A group of ten young people were playing a group game called "Pass the Message." The kids were standing in a row when the leader whispered a secret into the ear of the first person: "Johnny and his two brothers like to go to Jenny's house." Person number two repeated it to person number three as, "Johnny and his two brothers like Jenny, and they want to go to her house." The fourth person could not remember how many brothers were involved, so he said, "Johnny and his three brothers like Jenny," and omitted completely the part about going to Jenny's house. The fifth person changed the word "like" to "pursue" and whispered to the sixth person, "Johnny and his brothers are trying to pursue Jenny." Person number six, a girl, related to Jenny's problem and whispered to number seven, "Jenny's having a hard time deciding who to choose because Johnny and all of his brothers are pursuing her." Person number seven told person number eight, "Jenny has so many boyfriends she has a hard time deciding which one to date." Person eight told person nine, "Lots of boys like Jenny because she is a flirt." Number nine told number ten, "Jenny likes to fool around with guys." Number ten told the entire group, "Be careful with Jenny because she'll try to trap you in a relationship."

Clearly, by the time the message made its way around the group, it was totally different from what was originally said.

APPLICATION

Gossip

EXPLANATION

Most people have a hard time correctly receiving a message and then repeating it verbatim. Typically, we tend to listen with bias, adding our own perspectives (which are based on our own unique experiences

49

and background). Our memory is limited. When we receive too many detail such as dates, times, and names, the main point can be lost and we stop listening, thereby reaching a premature and incorrect conclusion. If someone tells us a story we are not interested in, we may listen only half-heartedly. Later on, when relaying it to someone else, we may add to (exaggerate) or leave out details, thus changing the context of the story.

Gossiping works the same way. By changing a word or by adding a positive or negative overtone, the entire message can change. This change can embarrass a person, hurt her reputation, and even cause permanent emotional damage.

Gossip is a destroyer. It can ruin friendships. Misinformation being circulated can increase anxiety. Rumors can cause a person to think the story is about him when it might be about someone else. Gossip destroys the trust and morale of any group or relationship.

In order for a person to be deemed trustworthy, he must absolutely keep all things confidential. Talking to others (gossiping) about anyone's private business is never helpful. Gossip always hurts you, the one being discussed, and everyone you talk to. There is, however, one Person to whom you can go with anything you ever hear. Not only will He keep all things private; He will also give you enlightenment and help you see things through His eyes. Talking to God about your friend's situation is the most effective way to help him or her because only God can change circumstances and human hearts to make a difference.

It is vital that we pray for one another, but remember that sharing another's needs can be a form of gossip. All details do not need to be revealed; God already knows the circumstances. Because we ourselves cannot heal or restore, it is not necessary for us to know all the details. It is only necessary for us to hold that person in love before God and entrust him or her to His care.

A Real-Life Story

For several years, Marian had attended a weekly women's prayer meeting and had grown very close to those in the group. One morning over coffee, Marian shared a personal health concern with Susie, a member of the prayer group. Marian had just come from the doctor, where it was discovered that she had an acute but treatable illness. Because Susie had always been trustworthy, it never occurred to Marian to ask her to keep the matter confidential. Instead, she assumed Susie would simply pray for her and that it would go no further. Marian didn't give it any further thought. The following Sunday at church, however, Marian was questioned by another prayer group member who was very concerned—and very interested in—Marian's "incurable disease."

Marian suddenly felt betrayed and oddly exposed. Keenly aware that she had confided only in Susie, she determined that no one in the prayer group was trustworthy. She determined that day to no longer attend.

What really happened?

As soon as Susie and Marian had finished their coffee and parted company that day, Susie got right on the telephone with her prayer group members and shared Marian's need for healing. In doing so, she embellished a few details, ensuring the story was juicy enough to hold everyone's interest.

In other words, she spread gossip about her friend. Over the course of the week, they all talked among themselves, each adding a little piece of misinformation until, by week's end, Marian's illness had grown into a full-fledged, incurable disease!

What does the Bible say about gossip?

In James 3:4–6, the tongue is compared to a ship's rudder, as a very small part of the body, and as a fire. Regardless of how small it is, it plays a very significant role in our lives.

*Or take ships as an example. Although they are so large and are driven by strong winds, they are steered by a very small rudder wherever the pilot wants to go. *⁵*Likewise the tongue is a small part of the body, but it makes great boasts. Consider what a great forest is set on fire by a small spark. *⁶*The tongue also is a fire, a world of evil among the parts of the body. It corrupts the whole person, sets the whole course of his life on fire, and is itself set on fire by hell.*

Likewise, in Proverbs 16 we read that a scoundrel plots evil (16:27) and his speech is like a scorching fire. Ouch! Proverbs 16:28

describes a scoundrel as one who stirs up dissension, and a gossip as one who separates close friends.

On the contrary, the Bible also tells what blessings will come our way when our words are tender and true. Proverbs 16:21 says, "The wise in heart are called discerning, and pleasant words promote instruction." And in verses 23–24 we read, "A wise man's heart guides his mouth, and his lips promote instruction. Pleasant words are a honeycomb, sweet to the soul and healing to the bones."

The next time you are tempted to spread a little gossip, remember the wise writings of Solomon, who wrote the Proverbs for our benefit. Choose your words carefully, and make sure they are sweet. Keep in mind that someday you may have to eat them!

In giving words of encouragement, you will reap a harvest of joy.

THE SQUIRREL

A squirrel crossed a busy street in a residential neighborhood. Halfway across, he stopped to rethink his decision: should he turn around and go back, or continue across? In those few short seconds of indecision, an oncoming car ran right over him, and the poor little guy lie dead on the pavement.

Across town in a different neighborhood, another squirrel darted across the street and stopped when he was safely on the sidewalk. But he immediately questioned his decision: should I stay here or go back to where I'd been? In a flash he bolted into the road, not even noticing that a car was coming. The driver braked, not knowing what the little squirrel would do, but it was too late. He hit the squirrel and killed it.

APPLICATION

Making decisions

EXPLANATION

With so many people out of work and looking for a job, Brad felt his chances of finding work were almost impossible. Although he sent out resumes daily, there were few responses. Depression was setting in, his savings was running low and he was feeling like a failure. If it weren't for his wife's job, he didn't know what he would do, and he toyed with the thought of giving up. But then one day he received a call from a company to which he'd applied for a job; they wanted him to come for an interview. He was so excited he could hardly sleep at night and thought of different questions they might ask him at the interview.

However, there was a major problem: the job was located several hours away in a neighboring state. Although Brad and his wife, Joanne, knew this, they didn't talk about the ramifications if he were to take it, even though they each had their own ideas about what would happen.

The interview went well, and Brad came home feeling confident. Still, he and Joanne didn't discuss what they would do if he took the job. Would she simply quit her job to go with him? Would Brad go on ahead and travel back home on weekends? What about their house? Would they sell it or try to rent it? And what about her parents who lived next door? Would they move, too, so they could be close, or would they all take turns traveling back and forth for visits?

All these questions and scenarios went through Brad's and Joanne's minds while they waited for the company to call Brad. One week went by, then two, and then three. Brad had almost given up when, during the fourth week, the phone rang, and the company offered him the job.

Wow! What a wonderful and happy day. He couldn't wait for Joanne to come home from work to tell her the good news, so he called her. However, she did not receive it as happily as he had, and an argument ensued. All the issues they'd been avoiding came rushing out:

all the fears, all the questions, everything. Later that evening and throughout the following week, Brad and Joanne fought about the decisions they would face if he took the job. It was hard for them to see any alternatives because they were so close to the problems.

Since so much time passed without the company hearing from Brad, they offered someone else the job. Brad had been tied up emotionally with all the questions and hadn't even realized that as far as this job was concerned, he was as dead as the squirrel that stopped in the middle of the road, unable to make up his mind. In this case, time was the vehicle that ran over Brad.

Herbert V. Prochnow wrote: "There is a time when we must firmly choose the course we will follow, or the relentless drift of events will make the decision. He who insists on making a perfect decision will never decide."

None of our decisions will be perfect because problems always follow. And *not* making a decision *is* making a decision. Hesitation can cause you to miss out on many terrific opportunities. If the squirrels had made up their minds ahead of time, they would probably both be alive today.

Fear of the unknown, such as whether or not to take a job far from home, can be scary. But the Bible tells us to seek wise counsel. A counselor could have provided Brad and Joanne with various scenarios of what some of the problems—and solutions—might be. By facing their fears and discussing alternatives, they would have been ready to make an educated decision based on facts, not feelings only.

There are many options in life, and sometimes you have to take a step of faith and simply trust that God will take care of the details. Let Him be in control of your life. When He brings you to a new step, He will be walking ahead of you. He will give you the best, not the second best, because He loves you so much. Let Him take care of the unknown details and problems that arise. If God wants you to take a step of faith and make a change, you can rest assured that he has a huge blessing awaiting you. He always knows what is best for you.

Now let's consider another individual who chose to accept a new challenge. When problems arose, she began to doubt her decision and wish she could go back, like the squirrel that crossed the street and then ran back to the other side. Sometimes these people blame God for the disruptions they encounter.

Tessa had always wished for a boyfriend—someone who would admire her and take her places. When she went anywhere, she felt like an outcast, as though she was the only one without somebody special. She prayed that God would help her find the right man. Then one day at college, she met Ben. At first, they were best friends and then they began to go out. One day they realized they were in love.

She was sure Ben was the one God had sent to her. They came from similar family backgrounds, would both graduate at the same time, and had similar interests and hobbies. The ways they were different offered opportunities to explore things out of their comfort zone. Both the similarities and the differences attracted them to each other, and they seemed to be an ideal couple.

Before graduation Ben proposed, asking if she would be his lovely bride and marry him. Quickly she said yes and a whirlwind engagement period ensued. Family and friends thought they were a perfect couple.

For the first few months it was wedded bliss. Ben could hardly wait to come home after work and be with Tessa. They spent time together every night watching movies, going for walks, talking, and playing. Meanwhile at work, Ben began to climb the ladder of success and was promoted to company Vice President before his and Tessa's first anniversary.

Business meetings and business trips began to take Ben away occasionally. Tessa started feeling more and more left out of Ben's life, and she started to complain. Ben was torn because he was eager to do well at work and enjoyed the prestige as well as the fat paychecks. On the other hand, he hated even telling Tessa because he knew the nagging would begin. Ben began staying later at work and Tessa's frustration grew by leaps and bounds. Naturally, they were growing apart, going their separate ways.

One day when Ben came home from work, he found a note that Tessa had written, saying she'd had enough and was tired of being ignored. She was moving back to her parents' home to be with them.

There is no perfect marriage. Once the romantic stage is over, problems will arise and need to be resolved. The characteristics that attracted Tessa and Ben to each other were still there, in spite of the problems. But Tessa had unrealistically expected the honeymoon to last forever. She wasn't prepared for real life to set in. Instead of trying to solve the issues as they arose, she gave up the marriage.

If they had gotten counseling right away, they could have worked on the problems and probably saved their marriage. Marriage is a journey through life, and married couples walk it together, like walking down a path. Along the way there will be stones—little stones, medium-sized stones, and big stones. Once in a while there might be a boulder. These stones represent crisis points such as a loss (a death, loss of a job, moving away from family) or a gain (the birth of a baby, getting a new job, buying a house). If the couple gets help when going through crises, they will be empowered to continue the journey with realistic expectations and valuable communication skills.

It is important to acknowledge each stone, or crisis, in order to continue walking down the path in a healthy manner. In Ben and Tessa's case, they could have proactively sought alternatives to have their needs met. Alternatives could have included setting time aside for a date, where they could talk, watch a movie, or go for a walk, like they did in the beginning of their marriage. Tessa could have found a hobby, a job, or a place to volunteer while Ben was away.

The above examples show that neither indecisiveness nor regret over a decision is a beneficial alternative.

If you face your problems and resolve them, you will feel like a victor. The choice is yours: do you want to be victim or a victor?

THE WINDSHIELD AND THE REARVIEW MIRROR

A teenager was taking driver's education. He sat in the classroom day after day, learning how to drive. The big day finally came when he got behind the wheel of a car to drive on the road for the first time. The teacher cautioned him to check his windshield and mirrors and make sure he could clearly see the road before proceeding. When the student got on the road, he was doing fine until he decided to change lanes, and did so without consulting his rearview mirror. He pulled in front of a car and almost got in an accident! His teacher pointed out his mistake—that he had failed to look in his rearview mirror. Nervously, the student concentrated on looking in his rearview mirror, neglecting to look through the windshield at the road ahead, and almost rear-ended the car in front of him! Again, the teacher pointed out his mistake. She explained that he must spend most of his time concentrating on the road ahead, looking back just enough to determine where he is in relation to the rest of the traffic. When the student found the right balance of looking ahead and checking what was behind, he was able to drive safely.

APPLICATION

Christian living

EXPLANATION

The path ahead of us is more important than what is behind us. Sometimes as Christians we regret our past so much that we neglect our future. Much of our future is beyond our vision because it is in God's hands. But whatever is within our vision is our responsibility, and we need to keep looking forward to make sure we are on the right track and honoring God in whatever we do or say. Keeping our eyes on the road ahead helps us do our part in creating the future God has in store for us.

If we spend most of our time looking in life's rearview mirror, longing for the past or regretting our past mistakes, we will be distracted, we'll create more problems for ourselves, and we'll have more trouble experiencing the current and future blessings God wants us to have. A car's windshield is bigger than its rearview mirror for a reason: it's more important to keep our eyes on the road ahead. We can't change our past, but we can shape our future by what you do in the present. Keep looking forward!

Penny got stuck in the past because she was unable to leave her past hurt behind. She was reared in a home where she was never given any praise. Every time her parents opened their mouths, it was to criticize. As an adult, she became her own worst critic. Not a single day passed that she did not condemn herself. When her son had trouble in school, she told herself that she was a bad mother. When a friend passed by her without saying hi, she assumed she must have said something wrong that had made her friend not want to have anything to do with her. In reality, her friend was merely distracted and had not realized that she passed her. When her husband innocently made a comment about the house, she concluded that she was a "bad wife." Any time she made a mistake at work, she worried that she would be fired and unable to afford food for her kids. She worried that her kids would become very sick. One day Penny had an anxiety attack. She thought she would end up in the mental hospital for the rest of her life.

She went to her doctor for the treatment of her anxiety and was prescribed medication. Her doctor also referred her to Dr. Rita for counseling. Through talking to Dr. Rita, she realized her anxiety was an emotional problem, rooted in her past. Through the shedding of tears, accepting her past loss, and forgiving her mother for the pain she was causing her, she was able to look at herself and her future differently. Like the teen-aged driver in the story, she was finally able to focus on the front windshield and stop staring through the rearview mirror.

For the first time Penny realized how much her husband and her children loved her. She used to keep a distance between herself and other people. She did not want people to reject her so she pushed them away.

As she learned to change her negative thoughts to positive ones, she was able to enjoy her present. She enrolled in an exercise program, began trying new things, and learned to set boundaries with others. She understood that as long as she focused on what she could do in the present, God would take care of her future.

The front windshield in this analogy is bigger than the rearview mirror. By focusing on what was ahead of him most of the time and looking in the rearview mirror once for a while, the teen could drive safely. What was beyond his vision belonged to God. In the same way, Penny expended a lot of energy focusing on her past. The truth is, she needed to look into the past only once in a while to get insight for her present; that way, she could spend most of her energy focusing on her present and trusting God for her future. Yesterday is gone; forget it! Tomorrow is not reachable; leave it! Today is here; use it!

COPING MECHANISM

GLASSES

"Beep, beep, beep . . ." Sam's alarm kept ringing until he finally pushed the stop button. Reluctantly, because he was very tired, he dragged himself out of bed. There would be no sleeping in today because he was to lead the 9:00 a.m. staff meeting that morning and it was critical to be on time. Without bothering to put on his glasses, he stumbled to the kitchen to make a pot of coffee, and then drew the curtain aside to peek outdoors.

Oh what a beautiful view awaited him. The sky was blue and the grass was green and everything appeared to be perfect. It looked as though nothing needed to be done. He smiled to himself and wondered what the neighbors thought of his totally awesome yard. For a few minutes he let his mind run away with those types of thoughts and then suddenly remembered that he needed to get going.

A few minutes later, he was ready to head out the door. Now he was wearing his glasses. His pin-striped tie was just right, and he admired the way he looked in his new blue suit. He ran his fingers through his hair and looked in the mirror again. With his briefcase in one hand and the travel mug of coffee in the other, he was ready to hit the road running, Sam was a handsome man and seemed to be the perfect husband. He provided well for his family, took care of his possessions, and made sure his house and yard were neat and tidy. He was a deacon at church and served on several committees. He always went above and beyond at work, too. As a result he had received several promotions. Everyone thought very highly of Sam, including himself.

He drew a deep breath and smelled the sweet fragrance of the nearby lilacs. Before getting into the car, he scanned his perfectly groomed yard but was caught off-guard by what he saw. Dandelions, about a million of them, covered the lawn. Some still had the bright yellow flowers but most were white cotton ball heads. *How could this be*, he asked himself. Why hadn't he seen them earlier when he was looking out the window? Then he remembered that he was not wearing his glasses at that time, and everything had looked perfect.

His spirit plummeted as he contemplated ridding his yard of those pesky weeds. He did not want the neighbors to think their yards were better than his. Sam was so annoyed that he drove aggressively all the way to work and even let it interrupt his thoughts once he got there.

It wasn't so much the dandelions themselves that bothered Sam, but more that everyone would see them and think less of him. If his yard were way off the road and hidden from view, dandelions would not be much of an issue, but it bothered him because he lived in a subdivision where everyone could see.

Can you relate to Sam? Does having a problem bother you, or do you care more that someone might find out about it?

APPLICATION

Addiction of any type, or any hidden sin

EXPLANATION

Some people live in denial and pretend that everything is perfect. Instead of dealing with issues that arise, they hide behind a career, church activities, spouse, children, or all the latest "toys." In this way, they create a make-believe world where nothing is real and nothing important really matters.

The fact that the dandelions bothered Sam so terribly was actually indicative of his heart, where something else, something sinister and dark, was hiding. By focusing only on the outside, he was hoping no one would find out what was lurking within. Just as he had seen a perfect lawn when he wasn't wearing his glasses, others looking at him would see the perfect man—the perfect husband, father, provider, and employee. But it wasn't real. None of it was real. Sam was living a lie, and sooner or later, God exposes all lies.

When Sam was a young teen, he found a girly magazine and quickly became absorbed in the dark world of pornography. It was a taboo subject at home, of course, where appearances were important and "things of that sort" were not discussed. His sin was ever-growing, ever-silent, ever-secretive, and it never went away. He hoped it would disappear when he got married, but it didn't. When he joined the church, he hoped it would go away, but it didn't. Instead, it grew and grew and grew until one day he acted on those desires at an after-work party. The affair lasted much longer than he thought it would, and now he was in a predicament he didn't know how to handle.

The truth was, he couldn't handle it because the affair itself was in control, at least as long as it was kept secret. More than anything he wanted to come clean and tell his wife—to have her forgiveness and God's—and at the same time, he intensely feared the consequences. He knew he could lose everything. So rather than owning up to his trespasses, he desperately tried to hide them by making a big deal about other things, such as those dandelions.

Sam did a good job hiding his secret life. He genuinely liked and cared about people, but by keeping busy he was also able to stay distant and not let anyone into his world. He thought no one else knew about the affair—only him and the woman. But there was someone else involved, a silent onlooker who loved Sam enough to intervene, and that was the Person of Jesus Christ, our Lord.

One day while coming home from his lover's place, a truck rear-ended Sam's car, sending him slamming into another car. He was taken to the hospital where he precariously wavered between life and death. It was there that he heard the Holy Spirit speak to him saying, "Sam, look inside yourself. You can no longer continue to live a lie and pretend everything is perfect. Others may not know what is going on inside you, but I do." Sam cried out to God, "Please forgive me for all the sins I have committed. Please give me another chance. I cannot pretend any longer that my sins don't matter. I will do whatever you say. Please give me another chance."

When Sam woke up a week later, his loving wife and children were standing next to him. He loved them. He cried and told his wife they needed to talk. There he confessed his sins, telling her about the pornography and the affair. He asked her forgiveness, and that moment started their new life together. It was very difficult for her. She had a thousand questions, and she struggled to do the right thing. Later on, after his recovery, he ended the affair and found a different job. He joined Celebrate Recovery, a twelve-step biblical program where Jesus Christ is acknowledged as the Higher Power. They sought marriage counseling and learned to communicate on a higher level. For quite a while, life was very rough between him and his wife, but they never gave up. They worked on the troubles they had always ignored and began to set time aside to be alone and get to know each other all over again.

Sam was sincere when he asked God's forgiveness, and God was faithful to do so, as He always is. The turning point for this family was when Sam decided to listen to the Holy Spirit and get rid of all the sins in his life.

The pair of glasses in the analogy represents the Holy Spirit. When He reveals our sins, we can choose to ignore His voice, or we can choose to be obedient and repent and let Him change us. At that point we experience relief and joy that otherwise eludes us. Living a transparent life without pretense is so freeing!

THE GRAY ZONE

Timmy and Lily were coloring a picture together on the same sheet of paper. Timmy was coloring his half with a black crayon because he wanted to show nighttime, and Lily was using a white crayon on her half to show snow. They were laughing and telling each other all about what they were doing.

Since no line was drawn down the center of the paper, neither Lily nor Timmy knew for certain where one side ended and the other began.

Without realizing it, Timmy colored with his black crayon onto an area that Lily had already colored white. Immediately an argument pursued. Back and forth they bickered, each accusing the other of taking more than their own share of the paper.

Suddenly Lily said, "Look, Timmy, when your black color mixed with my white, it turned into a different color that is kind of pretty."

Timmy exclaimed, "We made gray!"

They were each so excited and happy about mixing the black and white colors together that they forgot they'd been having an argument. They began laughing and giggling again while they continued coloring their picture.

APPLICATION

Negative thoughts

EXPLANATION

The type of thoughts a person has directly affects the way he feels and how he perceives life. Negative thoughts can cause a person to become depressed, angry, hurt, afraid, confused, or any number of other negative emotions. For instance, a college student who thinks that no one likes her may begin to feel rejected by everyone and then become depressed. A child whose teacher yells a lot might be afraid of getting yelled at next, and could even get so worried that he doesn't want to go to school. A gal whose friend hasn't called in a week might assume that her friend doesn't like her anymore, and then begin feeling sad and angry. A woman who finds her husband's cell phone underneath clothing in his dresser drawer may assume he has hidden it and is having an affair. A businessman struggling financially could entertain thoughts that his business will fail and that he could lose his house, car, and maybe even his marriage. An elderly woman whose husband fell down and got hurt could worry every day that he'll fall again and have to go to a home for the elderly.

In the situations above, each individual dwells on the negative, which in turn causes an overburdening of fear and anxiety. From one single bad thought, many other bad thoughts are born, each worse than the one before. Soon fears can take on a life of their own, and the person can literally become sick and paralyzed with worry.

These thoughts are called black thoughts. Thoughts that are negative, terrible, and fatalistic. They are unbalanced and unrealistic.

On the other hand, there are people who think nothing bad will ever happen to them. They think everyone likes them, that a failing grade is nothing to worry about (after all there's always next semester!), and that if there is not enough money today, that a miracle might happen tomorrow and they'll find a thousand dollars underneath a rock someplace. These are white thoughts. And while they do not cause a person to become sick with worry, they are just as unrealistic as black thoughts. They are Pollyanna thoughts—nothing-can-go-wrong thoughts.

These black and white thoughts are extreme because they are unrealistic. Yes, bad things can and do happen. And yes, good things can and do happen. Black and white attitudes are based purely on emotion and are not balanced by objective reality.

People who are healthy have thoughts that tend to be in the gray zone. For instance, when Joe receives a failing grade on a quiz, he realizes that he didn't understand the material and then studies that particular area a little more so the next time he'll be better prepared. Sue, whose friend hasn't called in a week, picks up the phone and makes the call herself. She understands that the phone works both ways, and if she hasn't heard from her friend, her friend also hasn't heard from her! These are two positive ways to look at potentially negative situations.

Sometimes it is not so easy to think in the gray zone. Take the woman who found her husband's cell phone, for instance. It would be easy to assume the worst, but what if that is not the case? Perhaps the husband lost his phone and didn't bother mentioning it to his wife. What would be the best thing for her to do in this case? Gently asking him would be a good start, but if he is really hiding it from her, and if he really is having an affair, then she would have to face that reality and deal with the hurt. But it is always best to consider things from the gray zone, the middle ground, and approach the situation with a positive outlook.

People who cloud their minds with black thoughts can become so fearful that they are no longer able to make decisions. Some people truly become frozen from anxiety! People who think only white thoughts are unbalanced, too, and could be in for a shock when they realize that some things really have bad consequences.

Every day, we all have the opportunity to think unhealthy, unrealistic, black or white thoughts, or to think healthy, balanced, gray thoughts. It is in the gray zone that we find peace and get enjoyment from life! The gray zone allows us to be in control of our own lives.

If you have trouble staying focused on healthy thoughts, perhaps you should make an appointment with a counselor who can guide you in your thought processes.

A Real-Life Story

Kyla was depressed because her house was a disaster. Dirty dishes were piled in the sink, the trash overflowed, laundry was piled as high as the ceiling, and toys were everywhere. Her friend Sally, however, was a wonderful housekeeper and kept her place spic-and-span. Every time Kyla went to Sally's house, she came home feeling bad about herself.

One of the reasons she thought it was impossible to get everything cleaned up was because she told herself she'd have to get it all done in one day. That is black-and-white thinking.

A balanced, gray thought would be, "If I clean for only one full hour each day, I'll have the entire house done in a week." This type of gray thinking is proactive and will put Kyla on the right track of getting her home all fixed up the way she wants.

Thinking should not be all or nothing (black or white); it should be balanced (gray).

Another area of turmoil for Kyla was that she had trouble finishing projects. All around her house and yard, things were half done. The flowerbeds were partially weeded, and the weeds she had pulled lay shriveled on the sidewalk waiting to be picked up; half-sewn curtains gathered dust on the sewing table, and grocery bags full of non-perishables needed to be put away. Bills and receipts were carelessly tossed onto the dining room table. Her whole life was a mess.

She thought of herself as a loser because she simply didn't know where to begin. Black and white thinking said, "I have to clean the sidewalk, weed the flowerbeds, sew and hang the curtains, do the dishes, and pay the bills. But it's almost 7:00 p.m. now and I'm tired, so I'll just watch TV tonight. Maybe tomorrow when I get home from work, I'll have enough energy to get it all done."

All or nothing . . . that is black and white thinking. It is overwhelming to look at everything that needs to be done and think you have to do it all in one fell swoop.

If Kyla had thought in the gray zone, she might say to herself, "I'm tired. It's 7:00 p.m. and I'm just getting home from work. This place is a mess and I can't possibly get it all done tonight. But if I work for fifteen minutes now, and fifteen minutes tomorrow night, and fifteen minutes every night after work, I can do over an hour's worth of work and will be a lot further ahead than if I don't do anything at all. On my next day off, I can work for an hour or two; in a few weeks, all my projects will be done and things will be caught up. I'm excited. This sounds like a plan I can actually stick to!"

Kyla's problem stemmed from her upbringing. Her parents were alcoholics and were mean when they drank, which was often. Being the eldest child, Kyla was expected to be responsible for many of the household chores, and when she fell short of those expectations, she was ridiculed and criticized by her parents.

It was a painful childhood. She had looked forward to having a different kind of life when she was older. Kyla's black and white thinking developed at a young age.

"I hate it here," she would say to herself (black thinking). "When I'm older, I'll have a nice home where everything's clean and new and shiny" (white thinking.) "My dad hates me," she'd tell herself (black thinking). "When I get married, my husband will love me forever and he will be my Prince Charming" (white thinking.)

Unfortunately for Kyla, she never matured from her unrealistic black and white thinking. At sixteen years old, she began wandering the streets and was taken home several times by the police. She was married at eighteen to an abusive man, the only type of guy she seemed attracted to. When that marriage ended, she continued getting into relationships that were harmful and abusive, and to this day is still living an unhealthy and unsafe lifestyle.

While this is very sad, the way she lives is totally her own decision. She has healthy options that she has not used, such as getting counseling to help her heal from her past and to learn different thought processes to make better choices.

How about you? Are you making decisions that are based on your feelings? Or are you making choices based on realistic expectations?

A RED PUNCHING BAG

A unique red punching bag sat right in the middle of John and Mary's living room floor. It was about three feet tall, made of plastic, and filled with air. The rounded bottom was weighted down with sand. When it was punched, the bag tipped over, but the sand in the rounded bottom always brought it bouncing back up again. It was amusing to punch the bag and watch it go up and down, and people enjoyed taking out their frustrations on the bag.

John was basically an angry man who would quickly become frustrated at anyone or anything that got in his way. For instance, when he lost his job, he was like a spinning, out-of-control tornado, throwing things in his rage, saying mean things to those around him, and damaging his relationships. There were many nights in the solitude of his home that the little red punching bag was pounded relentlessly by John's large fists. The bag always did its best to hold up to the beatings without coming apart at the seams.

Meanwhile, Mary was an emotional wreck from the years of John's verbal, emotional, and physical abuse. When he screamed nasty things at her and degraded her, she just stood there, quietly taking all he dished out. Once the storm was over, he would act like good ol' John again and expect everyone to forgive anything hurtful he had said or done and to never bring it up again . . . ever.

But Mary could not put out of her mind the hurtful words he had spewed, and so a slow burning anger smoldered within. She knew it was hopeless to fight with him, so instead she would yell at the kids and punch the punching bag. And the little bag tolerated the abuses from Mary.

Ross was the oldest child, and like his dad, he was often angry at things, people, and situations. At home, however, he was afraid of upsetting his parents with confrontation so he too would take out his anger on the punching bag.

While the nature of a punching bag is to be punched down and bounce back up again, it is not intended to withstand years of extreme abuse. As time passed, the little bag became more and more worn down until at last it had lost its air and could no longer stand up. It sagged sadly on the floor, deflated and useless. It had lost its purpose in this angry, dysfunctional family.

Because a punching bag has no feelings, it was obviously able to bear the abuse. But what if the punching bag had been an actual person, like, say, a young daughter? She would have spent her childhood being everyone's punching bag—both verbally and even sometimes physically. Would she have been able to tolerate the pain?

APPLICATION

Victims of abuse

EXPLANATION

Connie was the youngest in a family of four. When she was a child, she was exactly like the red punching bag. Her father, mother, and brother would take out their anger on her. To keep peace in the family, Connie would suppress her feelings and allow everyone to yell at or punch her.

She had learned this skill so well that when kids at school made fun of her she considered it normal behavior. Outwardly she looked happy, but inside she was dying. She had begun to believe that what her parents and classmates told her was right—she was a terrible person. She believed parents always told the truth, so she assumed she must indeed be bad. Since kids at school made fun of her, she concluded that she was a terrible person whom no one liked.

When she grew up and left home, she still heard the condemning voices in her head. In any negative situation, the first person she attacked was herself. She reasoned that everything was always her fault, regardless of the circumstances. She also learned to carry everyone else's problems. Her self-appointed mission in life was to fix other people's feelings. She tried to be nice and listen to their problems, but she believed she was at fault when anything happened to her friends. She tried to be selfless and let her friends have their way, but no matter how hard she tried, her friends would still get upset with her. She felt just like the red punching bag, allowing people to pound on her, all the while trying to be strong and stand up tall.

Since Connie had such low self-esteem, she married a controlling man who used verbal, emotional, and mental manipulation to get his way. After the wedding ceremony, it didn't take long before he forbade her to see any of her friends or family. He criticized her cooking. He rebuked and undermined any plans or decisions she made. Finally she just gave up and did everything his way.

Anger and shame burned within her, but she was afraid to tell anyone about her situation. She told herself that letting her husband have his way made her a good wife, but the emotional turmoil inside her told her otherwise.

She tried to be a people pleaser at work, too, but it seemed that her peers also took out their anger on her. Her children did not respect her because they were so used to having their own way and listening to their dad degrade her. When her daughter got into a bad relationship, she had no idea how to help her, for no one listened to any of her ideas. With stress from all directions, she finally had a breakdown and lost all desire to live.

Is your situation similar to Connie's? If so, you are not the one with the problem. It is those people who abuse you that are to blame!

Find a reliable therapist to help you process your past hurts. You may have to cry a lot and grieve over the loss of security in your childhood. You may feel like you'll never stop crying, but I assure you that you will stop. After you are able to grieve your losses, you will eventually be able to say goodbye to your sorrowful past and find yourself with a much lighter and much happier heart.

Gradually, as you heal, you will be able to see your current situation as it really is, and as it should be. You will begin to recognize when someone is trying to control or abuse you. In time you may find a connection between your current situation and your past hurts. With that new knowledge, you will be able to discern when someone is using you for a punching bag and be able to set healthy boundaries with people you love.

Once you are able to do that, you will begin to feel very good about yourself, and you will also find that others are beginning to respect you. You are a princess in the Kingdom of God! No one should EVER treat you badly! You don't need to be the punching bag for anyone ever again. With the proper help and guidance, you can learn to stick up for yourself, and you will feel absolutely terrific afterward. It is not too late to stop being someone's punching bag!

WHITE WALL AND BLUE DOTS

The painter had painstakingly applied several coats of white paint to the wall but still was unsatisfied with the job. Finally, in a fit of exhaustion, he sat down on the floor among the drop cloths and wet paint brushes and began to lament.

"What's wrong?" his wife asked when she came into the room and saw her husband sitting there.

"I've been painting this wall all morning," he replied, "but I just can't seem to cover those darned blue spots. They're everywhere. I'm so discouraged that I feel like quitting and not even trying anymore."

The wife closely studied the wall, trying to see the blue dots he was talking about, but there were none to be found. All she saw was a smooth, clean white wall, with no flaws; no imperfections and certainly no blue dots. In fact, it seemed perfect.

She told her husband that she didn't know what he was talking about—that there was simply a clean white wall. He insisted the blue dots were indeed all over the wall and he simply could not believe her. He slumped into a state of depression.

APPLICATION

Perfectionism

EXPLANATION

A perfectionist is someone who sets ridiculously high standards, both for himself and for others, that are way beyond anyone's reach. His way of life is to consistently focus on flaws and imperfections and tend to overlook any hint of success.

He does not enjoy the process of attaining a goal because he believes anything he or anyone else does is never good enough. When he sets a goal, he worries that he will not be able to accomplish it so sometimes he will talk himself out of even starting the project. Those who live and work around him become frustrated, too, because there is no way to live up to his absurd standard.

Take Mark, for example. Reared in a home with alcoholic parents, he kept the peace by walking on eggshells to avert his mom and dad from spontaneous outbursts of anger. He cleaned up the messes left behind from their drunken episodes, kept the house clean, the laundry done, and made sure his little brother was safe and cared for. In essence, at a very young age, he became the parent to everyone in his household.

Mark's life was out of control, and he desperately wanted balance. Not knowing how to attain it, however, he became a perfectionist, always trying to be the best at everything he did and expecting the same of others. Failure was not an option because he'd had enough of that.

Anything less than an "A" grade sent him spiraling into deep depression; he expected the house to be spotless at all times and the lawn to be immaculate. He mistakenly thought that these high standards were the foundation of a good home and could bring normalcy to his life. Striving for perfection made him feel in control of his circumstances.

Because he could not reach the perfection he desired, he felt like a loser, as though he had failed miserably. Instead of being a secure young man, he felt hopelessly insecure, afraid, and inadequate in all areas of his life. He was his own worst enemy and became exceptionally critical of others as well.

As life went on, he married and had a family and a good job. But the war for perfection raged inside him. Knowing they would be met with unkind comments and harsh judgment, his family and coworkers tried their best to avoid him. He longed for friends, but at the same time could not stand the thought of someone coming to his house and maybe tracking dirt onto the floor.

He became an isolated stranger in his own home. How disheartening it was for his children when he complained of their receiving anything less than an "A" on school projects. Just as he had done to himself when he was a young man living with his parents, he constantly criticized his wife about the house not being clean enough, the laundry not being done "correctly," and the mess she made in the kitchen when she cooked. She felt humiliated, unappreciated, and definitely unloved. It was the same at work, too, because everyone, including his boss, fell short of what he perceived to be as acceptable.

One day he mustered enough courage to seek help, and that is when he met counselor, Dr. Rita, who told him the story about the blue dots. With her gentle and loving guidance, Mark began to understand his need for change. He learned that he tended to focus on the negatives, or the blue dots, in life rather than the positives, a clean white wall.

One day Dr. Rita set a weekly challenge before him—to take a negative experience in the upcoming week and practice this new thought process. That opportunity presented itself the very next day when his son accidently threw a ball into Mark's beloved flower bed.

His first reaction was to berate his son, but then he remembered the challenge and instead decided to keep quiet, which was very difficult for him to do. His son waited for the abuse to ensue, but noticed that his dad did not yell but instead went into the house. It was necessary for Mark at that point to go inside and be alone to think about it. He told himself that his son did not mean to throw the ball into the garden—that it was simply an accident. Only a few flowers had been damaged (blue dots) but the rest were still in good shape (clean white wall). After pondering about it for a while, he came back to the family and tried his best to enjoy the rest of the day.

He could hardly wait until the next session to relay this "victory" to Dr. Rita. Over the months that followed, Mark continued to rethink the everyday, commonplace occurrences that would otherwise have set him off:

- After typing a report for work, he noticed he had made a typing error. Instead of focusing on that (blue dot) and retyping the entire document, he commended himself for having such great content (clean white wall).
- At his son's soccer game, he kept himself from yelling when his boy missed a goal (blue dot) and instead praised him for putting full effort into the game (clean white wall).
- When his daughter's glass of milk tipped over onto the dinner table, Mark refrained from screaming about the mess (blue dot) and instead commented on how quickly his little girl reacted and prevented all the milk from spilling (clean white wall).
- When his wife prepared a meal, Mark thanked her for taking care of the family (clean white wall) and said nothing about the messy counter (blue dot).

A neighbor stopped by to drop off something and afterward, Mark commented to his wife that the visit was pleasant (clean white wall) and said nothing about the visitor walking into the house wearing muddy shoes (blue dot).

Once his focus began to change from negative to positive, Mark noticed that his life became more manageable and in control. Not only were people starting to accept him, he was beginning to accept them. His family started taking time to be around him, instead of running away as they had done, and his coworkers began to talk to him once in a while instead of dodging into their offices and not interacting with him.

Mark was happier, and it wasn't because anyone else had changed; it was because he had changed!

CONFLICTS

THE COW

One day, Ken took his three-year-old son, Tommy, for a drive in the countryside. The green fields and bright blue sky made it a perfect day for a ride. Tommy was inquisitive by nature, and he spotted something he wanted to see.

"Daddy, could we go over there? I see something far away in the field," Tommy said.

Without hesitation, Ken replied, "Sure, let's go!"

Tommy had seen a cow, and he and his daddy looked at it up close. Tommy asked a million questions.

When they got home, Tommy told his mommy about the ride, about seeing the trees and the sky and the clouds and that he'd had so much fun with Daddy. Then he told about the cow. He said it had four big legs and "stuffs" hanging down from its tummy.

"Daddy said the stuff hanging down is udders and that is where milk comes from," he explained proudly.

Ken interrupted Tommy and, in an irritated tone of voice, said, "The cow also had a head, a tail, and a back."

Tommy began to cry. "No!" he shouted. "The cow only had four legs and a stomach with udders!"

Is Tommy's description right or wrong?

APPLICATION

Conflict resolution

EXPLANATION

Both Ken and Tommy each described the cow correctly. Ken stood almost six feet tall, so he could see the cow in its entirety, whereas Tommy, who was about three feet tall, was only able to see the cow's lower half. With that in mind, each description was correct—each according to his own perspective, that is.

When people disagree, they are often looking at the same situation from their own angle, or viewpoint, and often they both are right in their assessment. Battles ensue when people insist that their way is the only way. Continuing along those lines, they could fall into a conflict that has no resolution. And there they would stay, stuck in a lose/lose situation.

This is a free country, and everyone is entitled to believe what he chooses to believe. Two people do not need to look at the same situation with the same perspective.

How do we begin resolving conflict? Well, God gave us two ears and one mouth for a reason: He wants us to listen more and talk less. So often, people aren't willing to completely hear another's perspective completely before jumping in and adding their own two cents. By hearing a person through, you might find out that they are right and so are you.

Here's another story:

Jessica and John were on their way home from attending their friend's funeral.

"It's horrible that Tim died so young. I wonder what will happen to his wife and children. I feel so bad for them."

John answered, "If he had taken better care of himself, this wouldn't have happened. He didn't eat right or exercise enough and he was overweight."

Jessica lashed out, "Where is your compassion? This is why I have so much trouble with you. Why would you even say such a thing? Don't you care about his family? This is why I hardly ever feel loved by you!"

"That's ridiculous!" Tom retorted. "Why would you get upset at me for saying that? I'm just stating the facts. If he had taken better care of himself, he would have lived longer. There is nothing wrong with what I said."

They argued back and forth, insisting they were each right and the other wrong. The battle lasted for several days, and when they weren't yelling at each other, they were giving the silent treatment.

In this situation, both Jessica and John were right. John was correct in his statements that Tom's not caring for himself properly may have led to his demise, but he did not mean it to be critical. Rather he was coming from a rational, objective viewpoint. Like Jessica, he had also felt tremendous pain from the loss of his friend and great concern for what lay ahead for the family. Jessica, on the other hand, was way into her feelings about the whole matter and was expressing them. She was not looking at the "ifs"; she was only considering the here and now.

If Jessica had not reacted so quickly to John's statement, she may have understood that he was simply looking at the situation from another perspective. She knew he was a thinker and that he always looked at the facts, and she also knew that he did not necessarily express his emotions as readily as she.

In this situation, emotions were running high. John felt attacked by Jessica and quickly defended himself, which put Jessica on the offense. Instead of being logical during this emotionally-charged event, they both gave in to pride and chose to fight, defending their "right to be right." Unfortunately, this led to a dead end, with both parties losing the battle.

In another example, fourteen-year-old Daren was preparing to heat up some dinner in the microwave. He placed a slice of bread on top of the plate of food and covered it with a napkin before setting it inside. Right then his father objected, insisting that the bread should go in separately because the microwave would make it hard. Daren tried to explain that he was saving time by heating them together.

An argument ensued, with each declaring that he was right and the other was wrong. The son was angry with his father for treating him like a child, and the father was angry that his son was disrespectful by not listening to him.

Who was right—the father or the son?

They both are right. The father was looking at the situation based on his negative experience of heating bread in a microwave while Daren was simply being efficient so everything would be hot at the same time. Had they listened to each other's opinion, they would have discovered that both of their ways could work and may possibly even discover a third option.

Another example:

At a faraway church in the dead of winter, a discussion took place at a monthly board meeting. The hot topic was regarding the proper disbursement of a rather large and unexpected donation. One member suggested dividing the money equally among the various ministries so everyone would benefit right away, while another member thought it would be wise to save the money for unexpected ministry needs. The two bickered back and forth, each backing up his own idea in an effort to persuade the others to their point of view. The discussion went on for an hour without resolution. The meeting adjourned in a stalemate with a date to reconvene in one week to hopefully resolve this issue.

What was happening was the same as in the other story examples. Each person was seeing the same thing from his own perspective, without regard for the other. They each had the same goal in mind—to make sure the extra money was available for all church ministries. If they had quieted their hearts, opened their minds, and considered each other's perspective, they would have found the answer to be a little of both. They could have experienced a win/win by giving a portion of the money to each ministry right away, and saving the rest for future needs.

How many of us go through life trying desperately to persuade others to our way of thinking rather than trying to understand other people's perspectives? If we would be willing to hear another person out, we might find that he or she is also right. If we would take a minute to relax and accept another's opinion, we could possibly discover a third, and even better, option.

We are all different, and we all think differently, because God gifted us uniquely and He uses us in a variety of ways according to our backgrounds, personalities, and talents. We need to humble ourselves by allowing others to be right sometimes. By accepting that we and others can all be right, we open the door for many win/win situations.

How much better we all would be if we all could be winners!

THE CRACKED FLOWER VASE

A rainbow-colored vase adorned the coffee table in the newlyweds' living room. Flowers of pastel shades brought out the softer undertones in the glass, and visitors couldn't help but admire its beauty. Because it was purchased while on their honeymoon, it held special sentimental value for this young couple.

Years went by, and the vase became a common but loved household piece. Four children were born and the happy family grew. One day while dusting, the wife picked it up and examined it closely. She noticed that it had changed; something was different.

Looking at it from a distance, it appeared to be perfect, unchanged; but up close, it was clear that it now had many small cracks—so many, in fact, that it seemed it could fall apart at any minute.

Why did the owners neglect this valuable vase, purchased so long ago when their love was new and life was young? If they had given it the needed attention and care over the years, it might last another fifty years or so. Instead, it looked as though it wouldn't last another day.

How pitiful!

Application

Dealing with unresolved conflicts

Explanation

Brenda and Brian had the most beautiful wedding the town had ever seen. It seemed like a fairy tale as the carriage carried the handsome and highly educated couple to the reception hall. People looked at them in awe and thought, "What an ideal couple!" Their honeymoon was a trip to Hawaii, and it was there that they purchased the beautiful rainbow-colored glass flower vase. For a while they treasured it dearly because it symbolized the beauty of their life together.

The first year of their marriage was truly a dream came true. In their second year, Brenda was pregnant with their first child. After the baby was born, she found it difficult to maintain the house, keep up with her job, pay the bills, and take care of this beautiful infant. Slowly she began to resent Brian for not helping out enough at home.

Brian, on the other hand, was upset that Brenda was so preoccupied with the baby that she had no time for him. Quarrels became commonplace.

Every time they had conflict, it was like putting a crack on the beautiful vase. Their marriage slowly started to break. If one looked closely, they could see the wear and tear, but like the vase, it looked fine from a distance.

Time passed, and three more babies were born. Their lives were filled to the brim with busyness and became more complicated. Brenda eventually gave up her career to stay home and raise the children, leaving Brian as the sole bread winner. Providing for a family of six was stressful, and he worried constantly about making ends meet.

Because Brian and Brenda did not learn early in their relationship how to resolve their conflicts, they became like volcanoes ready to erupt. Surely their mouths ran faster than their heads, and hurtful words were tossed back and forth like a volleyball. The arguments, or cracks, accumulated to the point that it seemed their union might be unsalvageable.

Conflicts between couples are common, especially in the early years when they are learning each other's ways and finding they do not always see eye-to-eye. The important thing is to communicate tenderly and lovingly, yet clearly, in the differences.

There is hope for everyone who deals with conflicts. If Brian and Brenda's story sounds like your story, do not delay getting the help you need. Stop allowing more cracks in your marriage vase! Your vase, or marriage, is a beautiful work of art; don't ruin it with fighting; save it with effective and healthy communication!

FROM FINGER POINTING, TO A CLENCHED FIST, TO AN OPEN HAND

Bob and Lauren were an unhappy couple who continually fought and yelled and pointed fingers at each other, always ready to point out the other's wrongs. Bob belittled Lauren for living like a "pig," keeping a dirty house because she sat around all day watching TV and eating cookies. In retaliation, Lauren accused Bob of not being a good provider as money was always tight and there was never enough for extras. They had become so accustomed to the bad behavior that they seemed unable to stop.

Emotions ran high, and their finger pointing turned into holding up clenched fists. Realizing that they had become angry enough to start hitting each other, Bob and Lauren decided to walk away from the relationship for a while. During their time out, they each thought about how terrible the other was.

Lauren said to herself, "If only he would change, our relationship would be better. It would help a lot if he made more money, too. This is his entire fault!"

Bob told himself, "She makes me miserable. She's fat and lazy and being with her has been a huge mistake."

While apart, they continued to feed their anger by saying those mean things to themselves and to their friends. Doing so made it impossible to let go of their strong, angry emotions. They began to realize that when they pointed one finger at the other, four fingers were pointing back at themselves. In order to loosen the clenched fist, it was necessary to relax one finger at a time until the tension released and the hand was able to open up.

Application

Relationship, conflict resolution

Explanation

When people argue, each wants to win, and therefore, each believes that he or she is absolutely right and the other is absolutely wrong, and thus begins the blaming, or finger pointing. Each justifies that he or she is the right one and that the other is the one causing misery. If only both would make some changes, everything would be better. Unfortunately, even if one of them did make changes, the other would not be happy unless he or she was happy within.

Whether or not a person is happy is an inside job because happiness does not come from the outside. In reality, blaming and finger pointing can eventually turn into threatening with clenched fists.

Each person decides whether or not to unlock an angry fist. Anger is a choice. Peace is a choice.

You see, if you are the one who gets angry, you are the one to fix it. No one can take away your anger unless you choose to release it. Before pointing fingers at others, ask yourself if there is anything you are unhappy about. If you take charge of your life and get rid of those things one by one, you will feel better. Just like in the story above, the tension of each finger must be released before the hand can be opened and relaxed.

Changing someone else is impossible; it simply is not within your control! If you get into a relationship with someone thinking you will change him, but he doesn't want to change, then what? Then you are stuck! Changing yourself and your reactions to your circumstances are the only things within your control. In some instances, it is possible to change your circumstances as well.

If you are in an unhappy or struggling relationship and you focus on making positive changes in your own life, you will feel better. When you feel better, you can get along better with others. Has it ever occurred to you that it may be *you* who needs to make some changes so *your* life can be better? Thinking this way takes the focus off the other person and places it on you!

Here is a good example. Although Bob liked his work, he did not get along with his boss and worried about losing his job, which all added up to stress. With only a high school diploma, he knew another job would be hard to find. Add to this his anger issues (sometimes he would blow up at his boss, coworkers, and wife), and Bob was definitely in an emotional bind. Being stressed out caused him to have headaches, back pain, and chest pains.

The underlying factor was that Bob was very insecure and condemned himself for his mistakes. Knowing he needed help, he went to see his family physician and was prescribed an anti-depressant. Taking medication caused a deep internal struggle for Bob. He had always thought that Christians should have so much faith in God that they didn't need medicine. After reading scriptures, however, he learned that Jesus requested sick people to seek aid before He healed them.

For example, the scriptures tell of a blind man who came to Jesus to be healed. Before He healed him, though, Jesus asked the blind man to put clay on his eyes. After he had done so, Jesus healed the man. Bob thought to himself that since Jesus used tools (clay) to heal, there was no reason that he (Bob) could not use medicine as a tool to help himself.

At first, Bob did not like the side effects of nausea and heartburn, but after several weeks they diminished, and he noticed that his emotions had became more stable. He was able to think more rationally and make some positive changes in his life. Knowing that more education and training were the keys to a better career, he enrolled in classes to become a nurse. At home, instead of accusing his wife of being lazy, he began cleaning the house and organizing the closets. Since he was the one who wanted a clean house and his wife didn't seem to be bothered by the mess, he realized he needed to do the housework. In this way, he took control of the situation and solved his own problem.

Lauren also had a feeling of worthlessness, much the same as Bob had felt. She hated herself for being overweight, which had led to diabetes and high blood pressure. The doctor advised her to take medication, to exercise, and to stay on a special diet. Because she did not want to be sick or die, she diligently followed the doctor's advice, and over time, she began to lose weight and feel and look better. Her self-esteem escalated, and she bravely applied for a receptionist position at a nearby office. How happy she was when she was hired! Once she found out she was good with people, she felt even better about herself. Also like Bob, Lauren realized that she was the one who wanted extra money for the family, and she knew she had to be the one to solve the problem by getting a job. With a clean bill of health and the extra income, she was happier and more satisfied than ever before.

Bob and Lauren made changes of their own free will, and it amazed them that their relationship improved so dramatically. As Bob and Lauren grew together as a couple and as individuals, they argued less, were more peaceful at home, and eventually even went on vacation for the first time in years.

"For a happy heart, life is a continual feast" (Proverbs 15:15). When you find happiness within yourself, you will see the world as a happy place. Other people cannot make you happy if you choose to be miserable. Likewise, if you choose to have a joyful heart, no one can take it from you.

Has it ever occurred to you that you may be so busy trying to fix other people's problems that you don't have time to consider your own life? Do what it takes to make changes in your life so you will be happier.

MR. PAINTER & MRS. POINTER

One day Mr. Painter and Mrs. Pointer were looking at a picture together. Mr. Painter described the picture as having yellow flowers with a bee on the top of one, green leaves, and a river in the background. But when Mrs. Pointer looked at the picture, she saw only the yellow flowers. Mr. Painter says he is right and she is wrong, and Mrs. Pointer insists that she is right and he is wrong.

Mr. Painter and Mrs. Pointer decided to paint some rooms in their house. He was going to paint his den and she was going to paint her sewing room. They were both excited and chose their favorite colors. Mr. Painter put painters' tape along the baseboards, around light fixtures and trim, and on the edges of the ceiling. He painted the walls one section at a time, double checking to make sure he didn't miss any spots. Since he was sure about the color he had chosen, his main focus was to do an excellent job, without making any mistakes he'd have to fix later. Throughout the project, he did not entertain thoughts as to how the room would look when he was done; he only concentrated on the details.

Meanwhile, Mrs. Pointer went about painting her sewing room in a totally different way. She was so excited to get it done that she grabbed the first brush she found and never bothered covering the trim, baseboards or fixtures. The brush she chose was a hand-held flat, which she dipped right into the paint bucket. A roller brush would have eliminated the need for a ladder, saved time, and would have saved her arm and wrist from pain later on. She painted furiously, as though her life depended on it. Soon her arm and wrist were tired and getting sore, but she ignored the pain and continued on, determined to get the job done quickly. She was not at all concerned about details such as getting paint on the trim or ceiling. Instead she figured she could go back and fix the mistakes later.

Mrs. Pointer was an impatient, impulsive woman and could not understand why Mr. Painter spent so much time on tedious details. She wanted things done right now; instant gratification was always her top priority. Details frustrated her, causing anxiety and annoyance. She could not understand why Mr. Painter did everything so slowly.

Likewise, Mr. Painter could not figure why Mrs. Pointer was so sloppy with all her projects. The room she painted was a mess. Not only had she gotten paint on the ceiling and fixtures, but there were places on the walls that she totally missed, and paint had spattered on the floor. Because she hadn't bothered using the correct brush, she had to keep her arm in a sling while it healed from being overworked. This experience exasperated Mr. Painter, and the two were at odds with each other to the point of getting into a screaming match.

Mr. Painter and Mrs. Pointer represent two types of communicators: one who gets lost in the details and one who makes broad generalizations.

Mr. Painter is detail-oriented and loves to tell everything that happened, right down to the exact time. The details get so tedious that sometimes he doesn't get the main point. In the process, his audience loses interest. Mr. Painter doesn't notice that the listener's eyes have glazed over or that he is looking around the room, smiling and waving at others. Instead, Mr. Painter drones on and on and on, all to no avail.

Mrs. Pointer, on the other hand, doesn't like details, so she doesn't bother telling any of them. She assumes the listener will completely understand whatever it is she is trying to convey, and her conversations don't make much sense. For example, the church was having a fundraiser, and Mrs. Pointer was in charge of organizing the cake walk. She told the women that the event began at 11:00 a.m. sharp, and to bring a cake or two. But she didn't explain that each woman should bring a certain kind of cake (i.e. Betty should bring chocolate, Kendra should bring angel food, etc.), that they needed to be at the church by 10:00 a.m., and that they each needed to bring two cakes. This mishmash of information caused confusion as to how many cakes would actually be at the event, and women brought them in an hour later than they needed. This left bad feelings among the women towards Ms.

Pointer. They felt the cake walk event was thrown together in a hodge-podge sort of way.

When Mr. Painter and Mrs. Pointer try to communicate, they usually end up in an argument. Mr. Pointer tells way too many details and Ms. Pointer stops listening, causing him to get mad because she didn't hear what he was saying. When Mrs. Pointer tells a story, Mr. Painter doesn't understand because she leaves out so much information that whatever she says doesn't make sense to him. They often end up in a screaming match or giving each other the silent treatment.

APPLICATION

Communication, conversation, conflict

EXPLANATION

Here is a real-life story about James and Joyce, who have been married for many years yet have a hard time communicating. Almost every time they talk, they end up fighting. James likes to include all the details, but with all the information, Joyce begins to wonder what he's trying to get at. When she interrupts with a question, James becomes angry and loses his train of thought. Without clarification, however, Joyce can only guess at what James is trying to say. Her assumptions are usually inaccurate; this upsets James, and an argument ensues.

One day James had a particularly rough day at work and wanted to talk about it with his wife. Although he liked his job and boss, and the job was secure and fulfilling, all he really wanted to do was to vent and to get some things off his chest. He wasn't looking for any solution or help from Joyce—only a listening ear and a shoulder to lean on.

Joyce, however, didn't understand that he wasn't looking for help, because he didn't tell her. So Joyce, being a compassionate person, tried to ask questions and give advice. This upset James and made him feel as though she was pushing for more information and trying to meddle. Although he was telling her a story, he neglected to explain beforehand that all he really wanted was for her to listen. Because he

The Hippo That Fell Off the Seesaw

wasn't clear about that, Joyce began to worry that James was going to lose his job and that they wouldn't be able to make their monthly payments. She started to think that she should go back to school and get a job to help them get through. When James realized that Joyce had once again come to an incorrect conclusion, he became very upset and thought Joyce was looking down on him. Eventually, James decided that talking to Joyce was fruitless and decided to not even try anymore, especially when it involved his work.

In another incident, Joyce told James that she would not be picking him up from work that afternoon because she had to go to her friend Elizabeth's house. She did not bother explaining that Elizabeth's father had been hospitalized after suffering a heart attack and that Joyce would be watching the children while Elizabeth tended to her father. Because Joyce had not shared that pertinent information, James assumed that she simply had better things to do, and in so assuming, became angry and resentful.

James is a "painter" who plans and shares all the details about every situation without getting to the main issue. In order for him to more adequately convey his message, he needs to figure out beforehand what it is that he wants Joyce to understand. He needs to get more quickly to the bottom line, while still inputting some of the details.

Joyce, on the other hand, is a "pointer," and in order for James to understand her bottom line, she needs to add more information when talking with him. Because she has the details sorted out in her own mind, she forgets that others do not, and therefore she needs to delve more deeply into the reasons, or the why's, behind the main point.

James could help in this process by calmly asking Joyce questions before becoming annoyed or making an assumption. Joyce could help James by asking him to tell her the main point before going into all the detail. This would help her from drawing incorrect conclusions. If both James and Joyce try to be a little more like each other, their conversations will have a much better outcome.

God makes everyone to be different—unique in their own particular way. There is nothing wrong with being a "painter" or a "pointer" in communication. If James and Joyce can learn to accept each other's differences and make changes of their own, they will find more balance and become more forgiving and understanding of each other.

Assuming that your partner has a bad motive or is doing something intentionally to hurt you is usually a wrong assumption. Neither James nor Joyce has an evil heart towards each other or anyone else. It is their not giving or receiving enough information that causes the problem. Allowing each other to talk for at least ten minutes before interrupting could eliminate misinterpretation and conflict.

God loves you and your spouse equally. He puts unlike individuals together so that together they can see a bigger picture, make better decisions, and enjoy experiences they might otherwise miss. People with different personalities are able to raise children in a more diversified lifestyle and teach them to love people who are not like themselves.

God wants you to love your spouse unconditionally, the same way He loves you. This is difficult to do, but with His help and guidance, He will slowly transform you into His image. If you let Him do that, you will one day realize that your love for others has grown tremendously. When that happens, others will feel your love for them, and it is then that they will see Christ alive in you!

THE "POOP" FAUCET

Pat went to the kitchen for a drink. When he turned on the faucet, he was surprised to see stinky, yellowish, nasty water come gushing out. It smelled like sewer and particles of stuff he didn't recognize floated in his glass.

"Man," Pat said to himself, "this stuff is just like poop water." He dumped the toxic water down the drain and huffed off to work.

Tension was running high at the office that day—more so than usual—and Pat was finishing up a project when out in the hall a coworker began raising a fuss about a job he'd been assigned. Randy had always been cool-headed, but now he was mad at the boss and was making no bones about it. It was unusual for him to say anything unkind, so Pat was dumbfounded when a stream of vile language came spewing out of his mouth.

Pat wondered what in the world was going on and went to see. There was Randy, his face red, his fists clenched, and the veins in his forehead and neck popping out. Everyone just stood and watched, not knowing what to do. Then, as quickly as it had started, it was over and things returned to normal.

Although things now appeared to be calm, Pat realized that the mood of the entire office had changed. The spewing of those words and the harsh anger had left a definite stench in the air, just like the disgusting water that had come from the faucet that morning. Then it dawned on Pat: Randy's mouth was like a poopy faucet! His words were disgusting, stinky, and toxic and had contaminated the atmosphere.

Application

Conflicts

Explanation

Company was due to arrive in a week and Carol needed Richard's help to clean up and rearrange the furniture. She had asked him two weeks ago, but so far nothing had been done. She was getting annoyed and anxious because she wanted everything to be just right. Richard had a tendency to procrastinate, so she'd even allowed more time by asking him early on, but now she was reaching the end of her rope.

In her most irritating voice, she complained to him about his lack of caring, and Richard reacted like dynamite to a lit match. His face turned red and his eyes were like fire coming out of a dragon. He yelled at her for putting him down and said things that would have made his mother roll over in her grave.

Carol and Richard were now hurling insults at each other as fast they could, and their words had stench like the "poop water" that had come out of Pat's faucet. For forty-five minutes they lashed out, trying to outdo each other in meanness. They called each other names. Carol said Richard was a terrible father, and Richard told Carol she was fat. While they screamed and carried on, their little ones were crying and screaming, too. It was a mess. Even the neighbors went inside so they wouldn't have to listen.

This type of fighting had become a regular part of Carol and Richard's lives, and they didn't know how to stop. Every time they said mean things, it created a more toxic environment. Unresolved resentments built up, and neither learned how to constructively deal with conflict. If left untreated, their home would become sicker and sicker until no one would be able to survive there.

If Carol had chosen her words carefully and not nagged to get her own way, she may have been able to persuade her husband to help. If Richard had responded to Carol with gentleness, the day could have been saved.

The Bible says that our words give life or death. Proverbs 21:23 says, "He who guards his mouth and his tongue keeps himself from calamity (trouble)." If what you have to say will hurt or destroy someone, it is better to keep it to yourself. The tongue is a small part of the body, but it can destroy someone in a second. Choose your words wisely. Once they have been spoken, they can never be taken back.

In real life, what should a couple do when negative emotions arise?

One suggestion is to take a time out. Decide on a specific amount of time, perhaps fifteen minutes, two hours, or even a whole day—whatever is necessary. When the time is up, agree to sit down together and talk as calmly as possibly about the problem. The issue itself may never be resolved, but both parties should understand that it is okay to disagree. It's not whether or not you agree but rather how you disagree that counts.

During your time out, ask God to give you wisdom and understanding. He may change your thoughts, He may change your spouse's thoughts, He may change the situation, or He may do something else entirely. Be open to hearing your spouse's point of view. Remember, there are often several correct ways to resolve the same conflict. While you both may have differing opinions, you both could be right. If your conflict is solved, does it really matter whose idea it was?

Another suggestion for dealing with the energy that conflict brings is to do physical work. Gardening, bike riding, cleaning house, or going for a walk all use energy in positive ways. By turning a large chore into a project and working on it together, you could actually change the way the two of you relate. However, take small steps and rejoice in the successes you experience no matter how trivial they may seem.

In Carol and Richard's situation, it would have been helpful for them to sit down together and make out a list of things to do before their company arrived. Then, working together, they could have tackled the chores individually or as a team. In this way, no one would have nagged, no one would have been nagged at, and they each could have achieved a common goal.

Once you succeed in communicating with your spouse on a new level, why not celebrate the occasion? Maybe baking a cake and blowing party horns sounds a little corny, but who cares? Sometimes it is freeing to cut loose and let your husband or wife know that you still think he or she is the greatest.

And always remember to watch your words. Never turn on your poopy faucet! Let love pour from your heart and be a blessing to everyone in your family, especially when you're tired and frustrated. Kick back, and as the saying goes, "Don't sweat the small stuff; it's ALL small stuff!"

THE TRAIN ON THE TRAIN TRACK

The huge locomotive gathered speed as it descended the steep mountain. Dead Man's Curve lay straight ahead where the rails form a sweeping arch just short of a deep ravine. Many a train had met their fate right there. Conductor Ron began slowing the train, no small feat considering they were headed downward.

If he wasn't successful in properly conducting the train, it could jump the tracks and become land-bound, causing a disastrous wreck and possibly plummeting down the ravine. Everyone aboard would suffer terrible injuries and maybe even perish.

On the other hand, knowing when and how to slow it down would guarantee a totally different outcome. At the right speed, the train would cruise smoothly around the curve and travel without incident to its next destination.

APPLICATION

Dealing with conflicts between two people, Anger management

EXPLANATION

Dealing with Conflicts between Two People

When conflicts arise and tempers flare, people often say hurtful things and make misinterpretations. As emotions escalate, each adds fuel to the fire by making faces or gestures or by bringing up unrelated issues that were never properly dealt with. These flare-ups can be likened to a train running at break-neck speed down a hill. If not controlled, the couple will undoubtedly crash. In real life, too many of these crashes may lead to the derailment of the relationship.

Knowing that the argument is heading straight towards a terrible fight, each person has a decision to make: to continue on and let things happen as they are, or to call a time-out and take a break from each other. It is healthy to recognize when you are on a crash course and if so, to derail the situation before things are totally out of hand. During a time-out, deal with the energy of negative emotions through physical activity, i.e. taking a run or a walk or cleaning the kitchen floor, or by quieting down through prayer and meditation or writing in a journal. Unless you have a healthy mentor who will guide you with godly wisdom, now is not the time to call someone and talk about your problems!

Those who do not take control of the situation may end up using negative tactics such as the silent treatment, negative "humor" in daily conversation, throwing and breaking things, and even physical violence. (Negative humor is insulting someone under the guise of humor. It is not funny; it is very hurtful to the person and can destroy the relationship.)

After the time-out, talk only about the situation at hand and do not dredge up past arguments. Stick to the subject. If your spouse is wrong about something, and you have already stated your case, let it drop. Eventually he will find out for himself that he was wrong and hopefully it will be a good lesson learned. When that time comes, it is harmful indeed to say, "I told you so!" Instead, let it go. Remember, treat him the way you want him to treat you when you are wrong . . . because sooner or later you will be. In the meantime, do something together that you both enjoy. Reestablishing common ground brings quality time into your marriage.

In a healthy relationship, there is no room for pride, so put that down and treat each other respectfully. If something about work is bothering you, don't take it out on your family by getting upset about the dirty dishes (for instance). Instead, explain what's happening so no one wonders what he did wrong. No one should ever have to wonder. Keeping communication open without obsessing is like the conductor regulating the train's speed so it stays on track.

Stop the Anger

Peter was an angry, aggressive man. He had a chip on his shoulder and took things to heart, especially anything his boss had to say. Instead of being objective, he would be insulted and lash out, and eventually would either quit his job or be fired. This pattern ultimately led to trouble at home, and one day he decided to get counseling to find out what was really going on inside of him.

The counselor, Dr. Rita, learned that Peter had grown up in a home with an alcoholic father who would become violently angry for no apparent reason. At a young age, Peter thought of himself as a failure because all of his attempts in sports, academics, or relationships were met by his father's disapproval and ridicule. He "walked on eggshells" around his dad because he never knew what would trip the tirades, and he thought himself to be totally responsible for his father's anger. To him, anger and rejection were one and the same, with no distinction, and because he felt like such a failure, he thought he must deserve the constant punishment.

By the time Peter was of working age, he was ready to fight anyone in a management or authority position. He had no ability to deal with constructive criticism and, in fact, hadn't ever heard the term. At his first job, his boss told him to double-check his work before handing it in, and Peter interpreted that to mean what he had done was no good and that his boss was mad at him. Instinctively he defended himself by yelling and stomping off. Thus began the pattern of becoming insulted, fighting back, quitting, and/or getting fired, which was what had brought him to the point of seeking counseling.

Dr. Rita gently guided Peter to discovering feelings other than anger and how to experience them and express them. As he began to grow emotionally, his life stabilized and started to blossom. He learned about forgiveness, and then learned the process of forgiving—in particular, of forgiving his father.

The negative ways of expressing anger continued, however, because his reactions were such an ingrained habit. While it is one thing to learn a new habit, it is entirely different to stop an old habit.

Knowing he had played with trains as a youngster, Dr. Rita told Peter the story of the train, likening his out-of-control anger to that of a runaway locomotive. Peter was excited at the correlation. Certainly he did not want to be like that, like his dad had been, and he could clearly see the ramifications of letting his anger get out of control.

To remember the analogy, he taped pictures of trains on his desk at work, his dashboard, his bathroom mirror, and on the fridge. His wife even gave him a necklace with a train. The vivid mental image began to change the way he acted and reacted.

When Peter was angry he would feel intense energy, and Dr. Rita suggested he do something very physical at those times, such as running, taking a walk, going up and down the stairs at work, shooting hoops, or going for a swim—anything to burn off some steam. He learned that changing his behavior also altered his mood, a vital ingredient to his growth process.

Peter's life is no longer like that of a runaway train. Lasting change always takes time, but Peter has stayed focused on the goal of recovery and the outbursts have become less often and less severe. Today, he holds a full-time job in a factory and not only gets along with his co-workers but with management as well. At home, there is more peace and joy than he had ever imagined; the bills are paid on time, with money left over; and Peter is proud of himself for the tremendous growth he has made.

EMOTIONAL DISTURBANCE

CONQUERING THE CREATURES: AN ARCADE GAME

Sam loves to play arcade games, and his favorite is Conquering the Creatures. Snake-like creatures lurk within holes and pop out randomly. Sometimes only one will pop out at a time, and other times many will pop out all at once. To subdue, or conquer, them Sam has to smack them with a big foam hammer. The point is to keep them at bay by hitting as many as possible. The more he smacks, the higher his score will be. He hits and swats, constantly on the lookout so as not to be overtaken by them. Just when he thinks he has the game won, several come popping out. This game takes a lot out of Sam, both physically and emotionally, and in the process he works up quite a sweat . . . and quite a bit of anxiety!

He very much enjoys this fast-paced game even though it stresses him out. In the end, he's always relieved that it's over and he can move on to something a little slower.

If the game continued for a long period of time, Sam would not be able to handle the stress and could even have a breakdown.

APPLICATION

Anxiety, stress, depression

EXPLANATION

It is quite common for people to over-schedule their daily activities. For example Samantha, a young college student, fills her calendar with classes, a part-time job, dates, and sports. Lisa, a young housewife, fills hers by driving the kids back and forth to school, participating in PTA, heading up neighborhood BBQs, and being involved at church. Joe, an elder at the church, over-extends himself in various ministries, visiting the sick and shut-ins, attending meetings, and checking up on various projects and goings-on.

Samantha, Lisa, Joe, and others like them, believe that the busier they are, the more likely they are to be perceived as successful. But the sad truth is that their lives are spinning out of control, and when the unexpected happens, their worlds will turn upside down.

Everyone needs a balance of work, play and relaxation. Not scheduling down time (such as reading, going for walks, golfing, or taking vacations) could cause great physical and/or emotional stress. Physical stress can trigger headaches, angina, heart palpitations, dizziness, shortness of breath, and even heart attack or stroke. Emotional symptoms could include short temper, over- or under-eating, over-exercising or sitting around all day, over-spending or not being able to leave the house. These can all be indications of an out-of-control life.

Life has a way of happening and disrupting our plans. An accident, an illness, or something as simple as a friend dropping in for a cup of coffee, can throw our plans out the window and wreak havoc when there isn't time for anything not already in our schedule.

A healthy, balanced life consists of seventy percent work (this includes a job, taking classes, and housework), and thirty percent non-scheduled activities such as relaxation and play or an unexpected event. It is vital for everyone to have thirty percent of his or her time left open in order to have a balanced and healthy life.

Samantha, the college student, came to Dr. Rita for treatment of anxiety, where it was discovered that she had grown up in a work-oriented home. Idle time was never allowed, and if she sat down to relax, her parents insisted she get up and get busy. She was taught to never leave a room empty-handed, but to always take something with her on the way out (such as taking an empty cup to the sink or putting the telephone book back in its proper place). The parents rewarded the work-work-work mentality, but that out-of-balance life ended up causing Samantha to be an anxious, over-extended adult with vague boundaries.

Samantha made a daily to-do list, which contained fifteen to twenty items, many more than could ever be accomplished on a given day. Not finishing the list left her feeling guilty and a bit short of being satisfactory.

Dr. Rita coached Samantha to make an exhaustive, complete list of things that needed to be done, but she could choose only two things from her list to do each day. Samantha was beginning to relax, to have time for friends, for reading, and for anything else she wanted to do.

She learned to break down her studies into chunks, or blocks, of time. When she was unable to concentrate, she would get up and take a break for a few minutes. In doing so, she became more focused, able to learn more quickly and to retain more content than if she had continued to sit and laboriously study.

Lisa, the young housewife, came from a home where she was taught to put God first, others second, and herself last. While this is a noble characteristic, the entire family was out-of-balance and did not know how to rest and relax. As an adult, Lisa put others first by being overly involved in home and outside activities. Although each project was worthy, and she was good at organizing, she suffered because her own needs were not met. She had no balance—no time with God, no alone time, no time to read or write or focus on personal goals. She was tired, cranky, and frustrated but unable to put her finger on what was wrong. Her upbringing would not allow self-pity or introspect, so it never occurred to her that she was causing her own problems and needed to slow down. Her inability to always please everyone made her feel like a failure at home, in various organizations, and even at church.

Like Samantha, Lisa learned from Dr. Rita to incorporate the 70/30 percent rule and her world quickly began to change. At last, she had time to be alone with God, to spend time with friends, enjoy the kids, exercise, and rediscover her husband. Spending time with God and taking care of herself brought a zest for life that she had never experienced before. She carefully guarded her schedule so as not to revert back to her old ways.

Joe, the church elder, came from a home where achievement was highly valued. Coerced by his parents to be involved with sports, scouts, band, and other school activities, he never learned the value of down time. As an adult, he was very successful in his career and involved in many ministries at church. He wanted to take control of all the affairs at church. His life became so stressed that he had anxiety attacks in his meetings at work.

When he finally got to the end of his rope and met with Dr. Rita, she taught him the 70/30 percent rule. He learned to balance his seventy percent workload by reorganizing time at the office. He even discovered that people at the church did not appreciate him poking his nose into their affairs. Although this was a painful lesson, it caused him to re-evaluate what he was doing and why. As a result, he made better work-related decisions, and by minding his own business, was able to build stronger bonds with others and get even more work done.

Likewise, with his remaining thirty percent, he carefully chose activities most important to him, which were exercising and spending time with his wife and kids. At first, it was tough to refuse answering late-night phone calls from church members, but it became easier with time, and to his amazement he learned that the parishioners respected him more for setting boundaries and sticking to them. As a result, people came to him during the day when he was in his office, and he began treating the business side of the church work more professionally.

By following the 70/30 percent rule, Joe's life became balanced and peaceful. He and his family grew closer and even began playing games in the evening. Playing games had always been a no-no before, but he learned that there could be much laughter, and even healing, by spending this kind of time together.

Like Sam in Conquering the Creatures, we all need to take a break between each game. No one can continuously battle his or her creatures without breaking down and burning out.

Even Jesus needed time to relax. After He fed the five thousand with the fish and loaves, He quietly slipped away to have time alone with His Father. Being human, we need even more so to have our space, our alone time, so we can maintain that delicate balance of work and play.

HOW MANY BACKPACKS DO YOU WANT TO CARRY?

Amanda loves backpacks. Every time she finds one, whether it's when she's walking down the street, at a garage sale, or in the store, she simply cannot resist picking it up, slipping an arm through it, and wearing it on her back. It is not unusual for her to wear five or six at a time, even though her friends, family, and strangers tell her they think it's a bit odd. She is so engrossed in the present that she gives no mind to the thoughts and opinions of others.

It's not that she needs another backpack; she has one that fits her perfectly. It is the right size, shape, and color, and holds all the belongings she needs.

Sometimes the weight and bulk of all the added backpacks wears her out, both physically and mentally. They pull on her muscles and give her tension headaches, and her feet hurt from all the extra weight. At home she can't focus on the tasks at hand because she's dealing with all the bags; bags that she neither needs nor knows what to do with. By day's end she is exhausted, fatigued, tense, and even physically ill, and her family is getting fed up with the insanity of it all.

APPLICATION

Stresses

Explanation

One reason people get stressed out is because they take on problems that belong to other people. The problems, or backpacks, can be any number of things, such as trying to manage other people's responsibilities, trying to be everyone's friend, trying to take care of other people's feelings, or trying to solve other people's problems. At the end of the day, the backpack carrier becomes so exhausted from minding everyone else's business that he cannot handle even the smallest of his own tasks.

The key word here is "trying." You see, no one is able to handle anyone else's problems. God has given each of us our own portion, and those who are wise know to prayerfully consider what we have been given. When we want to help out but have much to do in our own lives, what should we do? We should go straight to our Heavenly Father and lift them up in prayer.

Now let's look at three examples of people who are attempting to carry someone else's backpack and the negative effects it has on everyone involved.

The People Pleaser Backpack

Tim was a "people pleaser" who wanted to win friends by "helping" everyone at work. When he first came to the company, he focused on doing his own job and he managed his duties very well. At the end of the day, he was happy and content with his accomplishments and went home to enjoy his family. Within a few months, however, he became overwhelmed with his workload.

The problem was that whenever anyone asked him for help, he always said yes. Oh, how he dearly loved the positive comments from his coworkers and the warm fuzzies he felt when they stopped by his desk to talk and ask for help. He felt important and respected.

But there was a huge downside to being the office big shot. Word spread quickly through the office that Tim would take anyone's unpleasant jobs and do them. Those little jobs accumulated quickly, and he soon found that he was not able to manage as well as he had been. He fell behind in his deadlines and the boss pressured him to get his work done. Instead of getting the friends he so desired, his coworkers talked behind his back and even called him a pushover.

At the same time, his home life was also spiraling downward and taking a negative toll on Tim's health. He had shoulder and neck aches, tension headaches, and was emotionally explosive. His wife and children were hurt from his angry outbursts, and no one understood what had happened to their once happy daddy and husband. Tim began to overeat and put on a lot of weight. When he went for his physical exam, he was told that he had type 2 diabetes.

Tim's problem stemmed directly from having low self-esteem and wanting everyone to like him. By saying yes to their requests, he thought he was pleasing his new friends, thus gaining their approval and having a sense of importance. In the end, however, he burned out physically, mentally, and emotionally, and it almost cost him everything. If he had continued to focus on his own responsibilities, his life would have remained in balance.

How about you? Do you carry the People Pleaser Backpack? If so, rethink your own boundaries so you do not become stressed to the point of breaking! Carrying backpacks that do not belong to you can be very damaging. God does not intend for us to manage anything other than what He has given us. If you find yourself trying to carry other people's burdens, remember to carry them straight to the Father's throne and leave them there! God will take care of everything in ways that are perfect.

The Rescuer Backpack

Lisa is a compassionate person who tries to save people from their struggles. When she learned that her sister and brother-in-law were having marital problems, she rushed right over to their house to "help out." She spent hours giving unsolicited advice as well as doing the cleaning and cooking and laundry. She thought for sure the family would be happier if the table was set when the children came home from school, so she bulldozed ahead to do that, too. She took on a parental role with her nieces and nephews by talking to them about what they should and should not be doing.

Lisa's plan backfired because she was intrusive and invasive. Her sister's family all became so angry for her lack of respect that she was asked to leave and not come back. For the life of her, Lisa did not understand what went wrong and became angry with her sister for her lack of appreciation.

Instead of rescuing her family, Lisa became a huge problem, and the entire family structure was strained to the point of breaking.

Lisa loved her sister and her sister's family and sincerely desired to do the right thing. The reality, however, was that God had already given Lisa her own life to care for. Sure, there are times to step out in love and lend a hand, but Lisa overstepped that God-given boundary and, in so doing, tried to play God.

God is our only Rescuer. He is the only One who knows all the details of everything and will lovingly help us put together the broken pieces when we turn to Him. The very best thing Lisa could have done was to pray earnestly for her sister and wait patiently while God did the healing work.

While Lisa was busy intruding on her sister's life, she was also a busybody in her own daughter's life.

When Lisa's daughter, Julie, told her about some problems she was having with her boyfriend, Sam, Lisa felt she needed to fix things by going and talking to him. By butting in and taking over, she robbed Julie and Sam of the opportunity to solve their own differences. Instead of standing up to her mom, however, Julie silently stood by and let her mom take over once again. By the time Julie announced hers and Sam's engagement, she had become co-dependent on her mom to take care of all her problems for her.

Wedding were underway and, as usual, Lisa took over and butted in to make sure things were done her way. Because intruding was what

Lisa did best, she erroneously thought she was doing Julie a huge favor. Lisa waltzed through the day, happy as a lark to be so busy with her daughter's affairs. What a martyr she was. But by the end of the first week, she was exhausted from trying to manage everything.

Meanwhile, Julie was silently furious with her mother's abrasive manner. But because she had never spoken up for herself, Julie's anger mounted, and one day she came unglued. An ugly fight followed.

Once again, Lisa did not understand why all her efforts were being discarded. As usual, instead of seeing that she might be part of the problem, she retaliated by getting mad at Julie and Sam for not holding their tongues. After all, wasn't she (Lisa) paying for the wedding? How ungrateful could those two possibly be? It didn't take long before all the family members chose sides, and everyone got caught in the uproar all because Lisa tried to live Julie's life for her and put her nose where it didn't belong.

Can you imagine how chaotic Lisa's life was? She was such a busybody that she didn't even realize she wasn't taking care of her own business. Oh sure, the laundry was done, the house was clean, and the yard looked lovely, but the emotional and spiritual needs of each person in the household were not being met. Resentment grew toward Lisa. There were undercurrents of hostility and overtones of negative humor. And all that stress took a toll on Lisa's declining health—back, neck, and shoulder pain, headache, insomnia, and stomach problems. She felt like no one cared for her even though she "helped" so many people.

How about you? Do you find it necessary to involve yourself in problems that are not your own? Do you gossip and tell people all that you've heard? Do you stir the pot, so to speak, of discontentment, trying to make yourself important in ways that are actually detrimental?

If so, and you sincerely want to help others, ask yourself this question: "Is this my problem?" If it is not, don't take it on. Instead, give emotional support by being a good listener. If someone's feelings are being understood, he is more likely to make healthy decisions on his own. Give spiritual support by faithfully praying. You cannot and should not try to live someone else's life.

Letting go will free you up to take care of yourself, and it will give God the room He needs to move directly in others' lives and in yours, too.

The Co-Dependent Backpack

Melissa was brought up in a home with a mean, alcoholic father and a mother who defended him no matter what he did. Melissa was her dad's caregiver and her mother's housemaid, and to her little brothers and sisters, she was their "safe" mom, the one they trusted when they needed nurturing. Erroneously, she thought that if she was a "good girl," her parents would not get upset. Even though that was proven time and again not to be true, she held to the conviction and carried it with her into adulthood. She always thought if she was good enough, she could make everyone happy. That unhealthy and untrue thought propagated another—that if she was NOT good enough, everyone would be unhappy. She did not realize that she was powerless over the feelings of others. Unfortunately, she thought that everyone's happiness or unhappiness was a direct result of her actions.

After she grew up and got married, she became overly anxious about her husband's feelings. If he expressed irritation, she assumed he was irritated with her. If he was jovial, she assumed he was happy because of her. When her grown children confided their problems to her, she soaked it all in and could not sleep for nights on end. A close friend, Janie, told her that she had cancer. Melissa took that all in and began to feel depressed as well as anxious and fearful. If someone at church acted a bit stand-offish, Melissa took it personally and wondered what in the world she may have done to make them behave that way.

These types of thoughts are non-productive and create a stressful life. Nobody has the ability to make anyone feel anything. People feel different things at different times, and while we may be able to guess how a person will react, we do not have the power to know or to make him react a certain way. While it is true that our actions can influence others, we do not have the power to control anyone.

Are you someone who thinks that your actions have the power to positively or negatively control others? If so, don't be surprised if you are feeling really stressed out! Remember, too, that your physical health is directly related to your mental health.

If you carry the backpack of a codependent, understand that you do not have to be a caretaker. God has given you a life—thoughts, feelings, likes, dislikes, hopes, dreams, loved ones, etc., and He trusts you to do your best with it all. He wants you to enjoy your life and to enjoy Him.

When you feel the urge to take care of someone, tell God all about it. You are not able to go into a person's innermost being to get to the root of the problem, but God is more than able. And He loves your friends and family even more than you do. Take them to God's throne and ask Him to give them what He knows they need. He always will.

Then you will be free to get on with your life and the cares that are truly yours. You will have a lighter heart and a happier disposition when you carry your own cares and leave the cares of others at His throne.

If any of these types of problems plague you, and you need further encouragement, find a Christian counselor who will help you along this journey. A professional therapist who loves God will be able to help you reestablish some strong, healthy core beliefs and get you going on the right track. "In quietness and trust is your strength" (Isaiah 30:15). Rest in the Lord. Place your burdens into God's hands, and leave others' burdens to Him, too. Let go and let God. "Cast all your anxiety on him because He cares for you" (1 Peter 5:7).

THE HEALING POWER OF WILLOW

Bobby wanted to have a little puppy when he was six. He dreamed about it day and night, but his parents kept giving excuses not to get

The Hippo That Fell Off the Seesaw

it. The more he was reminded he could not have it, the more desperately he wanted it. Since his parents kept saying no to him, he eventually gave up the idea and channeled his energy taking care of his hamsters.

One summer day, he came home from summer camp and found a package by the door. It was a gift from his grandparents for his ninth birthday. Bobby opened it up. To his surprise, there was a little puppy inside the box. Mommy told him that since he was older now, he should be able to take care of the puppy on his own. She made him promise that he would feed, walk, and bathe the dog since both she and Daddy had full-time jobs and had no time to care for the animal.

Of course, Bobby promised his mother without hesitation. His dream had come true and he could not wait to tell everyone about it. He named the dog Willow because it had long fur that hung to the floor and reminded him of a willow tree.

To his parents' surprise, Bobby kept his promise. He was excited to come home every day right after school because he missed his dog so much. Since Willow had come into his life, he no longer was afraid to be alone in the house after school. Every day Willow would stand by the window, eagerly awaiting Bobby's arrival. As soon as she saw Bobby walking down the street, she would start barking and running like crazy all over the house. When Bobby opened the door, Willow would jump and climb all over him. After having his after-school snack, Bobby would let Willow outside, and he would run after her. They would run and laugh until they were exhausted, then they would lie down on the grass by the creek. Now every day was a special day because of Willow. She brought joy to the entire family. Everyone adored her, and she quickly became one of the family.

Two years later, Bobby got a phone call from his grandparents that they were coming to visit. Of course, Bobby gave Willow a bath. He could not wait to show her off to them. When Bobby heard his grandparents' car coming down the hill and around the corner, he and Willow ran out to meet them. But right then, Willow saw a bird and immediately chased after it, completely unaware of the oncoming car. The driver slammed on his brakes—but it was too late, and Willow lay lifeless on the pavement. Bobby screamed so loudly it seemed the entire neighborhood could hear him.

Bobby picked her up and held her tightly in his arms. In those few seconds, time seemed to stand still. Bobby was so grief-stricken that he was unable to eat or sleep. His special buddy was gone forever. The whole family was very sad. They decided to bury Willow by the creek where she and Bobby used to play.

Bobby just could not get over the hurt and pain caused by the loss of Willow. For a long time, Bobby was so sad that he no longer went out to the back yard to play. Willow was gone forever.

APPLICATION

Grieving the loss of a pet

EXPLANATION

There are seven stages of grief, and everyone who experiences the death of a loved one, be it a pet or a human being, must go through all the stages in order to heal emotionally. There is no particular order, and sometimes a person will go through one or two of the stages more than once. Sometimes a person may feel as though he has done all the grieving possible when a sudden memory causes him to slip right back into crying or sadness.

In Bobby's case, he was shocked when Willow died. For a long time, he refused to believe that Willow was no longer around. He told himself that this was just a nightmare and that she really hadn't been hit by a car. (Shock and Denial Stage) He felt guilty that he did not keep her inside the house while waiting for his grandparents' arrival and blamed himself for her death. (Pain and Guilt Stage) Anger grew hot inside his belly, and he seemed to hate the whole world. He was angry at the driver who hit Willow; he was angry at his grandparents for giving the dog to him; he was angry at his parents for any chores they asked him to do; he was mad at his teacher for giving homework; he was furious when his friend would not let him borrow a game. But most of all, he was blaming himself for the death of Willow. He tried bargaining with God to see if there was any way He would bring Willow back to him. (Anger and Bargaining Stage) Months after of the death of Willow, people had stopped talking about her because they thought Bobby should be over the grief by now. Instead, he cried almost every night and sometimes during the day. He isolated himself and became very lonely. He thought about the good times he had had with Willow. Encouragement and comfort from others did not seem to help. He just needed to cry. (Depression Stage) "Blessed are those who mourn for they shall be comforted" (Matthew 5:4).

As time passed, Bobby's parents continued to make sure his physical needs were met by providing him healthy, nutritious food and a comfortable bed. To meet Bobby's emotional needs, they listened to him, talked with him, and sometimes even cried with him. His parents also made sure he was connected with his friends. Allowing his friends to come for sleepovers was part of their routine, and the boys would often go out to the back yard to play. That way, new memories were made that did not include Willow, and this was very healthy for Bobby. (Upturn Stage) Bobby's parents were delighted to see their son's progress in the grieving process.

One weekend while Bobby and his parents were walking in the woods, Bobby found one of Willow's toys and he began crying uncontrollably. He not only felt sad that Willow was no longer there, but he was mad and began anew to blame himself for her death (repeat of Anger and Depression Stage). But this time, Bobby did not stay angry and sad for long; instead he decided to put together a memory book of Willow. He used pictures and wrote captions underneath to explain what was happening in the picture and to express his feelings. When it was complete, his parents had it turned into a book. Bobby still missed Willow at times, but he became involved with sports and his friends and was getting on with life without Willow. (Reconstruction Stage)

One day a couple of years later, Bobby and his friends went out to the creek where Willow was buried. To their surprise, they saw a stick with leaves poking through the ground. Bobby ran to tell his parents to come out. After a little investigating, his dad determined that it was indeed a little willow tree. Since there were willows across the creek, the seed of one had planted itself right on the place where Willow was buried. It grew to become the largest willow tree in the woods.

Willow was still alive!

ROLLER COASTER RIDE

You and your friends have been waiting in line for half an hour to ride the roller coaster, and now it's time. Everyone's excited, scared, anxious, and laughing all at once. You all climb in and sit down; the bar comes down and locks tightly; with a jerk the ride begins.

The coaster lurches forward and slowly rounds a curve. At the base of the first and largest hill, a chain catches underneath and pulls it up. Higher and higher it goes. This incline is so steep it scares you to even look at it, but you can't help yourself. Jerk, lunge. Jerk, lunge. The machine slowly and noisily makes its way to the top. You're now above the tallest buildings and people below look like little ants walking around.

Some daredevils lift their hands above their heads as proof that they are not afraid. Others clamp their jaws together so tightly it seems their teeth might break. Still others hang onto the bar across their laps for dear life while closing their eyes as tightly as possible.

The coaster peaks, and the first car slinks ever so slowly over—then the second car, then the third, making the passengers feel like they are dangling in mid-air. Clearly they see the steep drop awaiting them. Few hands are now raised above heads as the reality of the drop sets in—even though later these same riders will tell of how brave they were. The truth is, everyone is gripped with fear!

In a split second the coaster races to the bottom at lightning speed. People scream in terror. Some open their eyes to peek but quickly hunker back down in horror. Before the last car even reaches the bottom, the coaster is already ascending another hill. Those who are terrified wish they'd never gotten on and already wonder if it will ever end. The coaster races around curves high in the air and then mercilessly plunges to the depths.

The terrifying ride lasts under three minutes and comes to a screeching halt at the same spot where it began. Riders are instructed to exit quickly and leave the platform. With adrenaline racing through their veins, everyone talks at once, telling his own story and rushing toward the next ride.

Application

Stress, anxiety, depression, relaxation

Explanation

Sometimes life hits us fast with an unforeseen problem then, just as quickly, slams us again before we ever have time to recoup from the first. It can feel just like being on a roller coaster. After we plunge to the bottom of that first big hill, we're already on our way up the second. These inclines and valleys in our lives can come in the form of receiving an unexpected bill, having a car accident, breaking a bone, or finding out you are pregnant. When faced with prolonged stress, you could begin to experience headache, muscle tension, fatigue, depression, anxiety, stomach upset, sleep disturbance, diarrhea, and many other types of physical and emotional problems.

Chad provides us with a good example of living life on a roller coaster. A hard-working attorney trying to get to the top, Chad is a co-dependent people pleaser. He strives to make his clients happy by meeting all their demands—whether reasonable or unreasonable.

He puts in countless hours copying documents, writing and rewriting letters, checking his messages, and returning calls. He meets with clients on Sundays when he'd rather be home; he sometimes leaves his wife and friends during special outings so that he can take important calls from clients. Even while on vacation, Chad ponders the problems of his clients.

All this work-related activity keeps his mind busy and his body tense. He has no real down time. As a result, he suffers with headaches, fatigue, and weight loss. Slowly Chad begins to realize that he is actually angry at himself for being used by unappreciative clients and decides to take control of his life.

The first thing he does is to hire an office manager begin taking only those cases he feels confident would be productive. Instead of taking and making calls and e-mails throughout the day, he designates set hours for that, which to his surprise frees up a significant amount of time.

One day on a whim, Chad left the office at lunchtime and strolled through the downtown area. On his return, he was pleasantly surprised not only to realize how relaxed he was but also that he was more productive the rest of the afternoon. He then determined to leave the office every day during the lunch hour and instructed the office manager to not work during her lunchtime. In the beginning, he left his phone on his desk so he wouldn't be tempted to take calls, but as he gained control, he sometimes took his phone with him and called his wife for a short chat. They would schedule a weekly lunch date at their favorite restaurant, and he began intently reconnecting with her. They also started exercising three nights a week at 6:30 p.m., so on those nights would leave the office by 6:00. He then made another decision. Whether he was exercising or not, he would leave the office every night at 6:00 and call it a day.

Are you like Chad was? Are you going from one activity to another without taking a break? Is your mind racing, always thinking of what to do next and never really enjoying the moment? If so, consider the following relaxation techniques:

Take up a hobby. Getting involved in a casual activity (one you are not going to try to master) can be most relaxing because you won't have expectations of a perfect outcome. Take up painting, study auto mechanics, make jewelry, or learn to knit. You don't necessarily have to be artistic or mechanically inclined; you just need to relax and enjoy the process.

Take a break from electronics. Turn off the phone ringer and let people leave messages. Check email and voice mail only during a designated time of day. When the time is over, stop and deal with them the next day.

Turn on the music. You don't need to be good at singing or playing an instrument to make music. You can simply drum a rhythm by banging on pots and pans, by blowing into bottles to make whistling sounds, or by humming. The Psalms instruct us to make a joyful noise to the Lord with singing and shouting, but we are never told the song or noise has to be beautiful; it only has to be joyful. So crank up the music and get loud and joyful!

Giggle and laugh. Read comics, cut out your favorite chucklers, subscribe to Funny Times, watch a funny movie. Go out and smile at people and watch to see if they will smile back at you.

Take a mental health day. When life is overwhelming, take a day off. Spend time babying yourself by sleeping in, wearing your pajamas all day, eating your favorite food, watching game shows, or by simply doing nothing.

Forgive and let go. It is perfectly all right to write a letter to someone who has offended you, and then not mail it. After you have written down everything you'd like to say, read it out loud, as though the person were in the room with you. Yell sometimes! Make it real, the way you really feel inside. If you cry, that is okay and healthy. When you're finished, you can either burn the letter or tear it up into a million pieces and throw it away. Make sure you don't read it again, but totally destroy it after you are done. It is sometimes hard to forgive, but it is more stressful to hold on to grudges.

Be a child. Take time out to play! Slide down snowy hills on a sled, build a snow fort or a sand castle, eat with your hands, go to the zoo, or visit a circus. You can do this alone or with a child, but enjoy your time and keep it simple.

Be with nature. Take a walk and look at the details of the trees and flowers. Breathe deeply and smell the outdoor air and the fragrant flowers. Listen to the birds and the rustle of the wind in the trees. Did you know that God created all of nature simply for our enjoyment? When you slow down and take notice of the wonders He has done, you are pleasing Him!

Relaxation spot. Make a comfortable place for yourself by moving your favorite chair in front of your favorite window. Surround yourself with books you love, comfy pillows, a journal and a good pen, soft lighting, calming music, and fresh flowers or healthy plants. (If you have plants that are half-dead, get a new one for this area!) This will be your own little place of respite where you can daydream, read, journal, watch nature from inside, and talk to God.

Find a sounding board. Talking to someone to let off steam rather than keeping your stress bottled up can help release some of your stress. Be sure to find a friend who is supportive rather than judgmental and controlling—someone who can accept your feelings and help you see the other side of things and point out that your situation may not as bad as you think it is.

Bake and cook. Baking and cooking your favorite foods can be a great stress reliever as you focus on something that will bring pleasure in the end. You can save it for your family or divide it up and share it with a friend.

Take a deep breath. Slow and deep breathing ten times in a row will help you relax. Imagine yourself sitting on the top step of ten steps. Breathe in slowly, hold it a second or two, and then slowly exhale. Now visualize that you are on step nine. Again, breathe in slowly, hold it a second or two, and then slowly exhale. Visualize that you are on step eight. Repeat this process again and again until you reach the bottom. Now, sit a minute with your eyes closed and your muscles relaxed. Slowly stretch your arms above your head and rotate them around in a circle. Stretch your legs. Breathe deeply once more, hold it, and exhale. Now you are ready to face life again.

Since Chad took control of his life and learned to relax, he has ridded himself of almost all the unnecessary stress baggage he was lugging around. If you are under any type of stress, you may need to regulate your lifestyle and make some healthy changes. A little stress once in a while can be good because it heightens physical and psychological awareness and leads to peak performance, but long periods of stress are like the roller coaster ride, racing from one fall to the next, affecting physical, emotional, mental, and spiritual abilities.

Psalm 46:10 instructs us to "Be still and know that I am God."

THE TWILIGHT ZONE

The morning sky turned pink as the sun peeked over the horizon. Birds chirped and sang, and sunlight streamed through the bedroom window. It was time for Mark to rise and shine and begin a brand new day.

Although he went to bed on time, he had tossed and turned throughout the night, and now was utterly exhausted. He hit the snooze button and buried himself under the covers, trying to shut out the morning and all its cheeriness. But just as had happened before he went to sleep, those relentless, undesirable thoughts crashed in on him like waves slamming onto the shore, and he seemed powerless to stop them. Would he ever escape from this living, hellish nightmare?

Mark was a church-going, hard-working family man who kept himself busy with lots of activity. The busyness kept him focused and gave him a sense of self-control. He read the Bible, loved his wife and children, and strived always to do the right thing.

It was at night, after a long day, when he was tired and vulnerable, that the thoughts would take over. He had sexual fantasies that were both pleasing and repulsive at the same time. These thoughts seemed to have a life of their own. They didn't make any sense, yet they screamed at him, and they felt very real. He desperately wanted them to go away, but he had no one to talk to, no one he thought would understand what was happening, and he didn't want to lose the respect of his fellow man, or his wife.

What he would give for peace . . . and a good night's sleep.

Is there any hope for Mark? His daytime actions and his nighttime thoughts seem to be opposite each other. Is he living a lie?

APPLICATION

Anxiety, depression, sexual addiction, or other issues

EXPLANATION

A "twilight zone" occurs during those times when a person is half awake and half asleep. It could be that time period when a person first wakes up in the morning and tries to go back to sleep, or when a person goes to bed at night and has trouble falling asleep. It can even occur when a person is waking up from an afternoon nap or is fighting off sleep during the day.

Worries and other disturbing thoughts tend to creep into our minds during these twilight times when our defenses are down. It is a vulnerable time, especially for those struggling with anxiety, depression, sexual addiction, and the like.

One good way to stay clear of the morning twilight zone is to get up as soon as the alarm goes off. Lying in bed to try to catch a few more Z's can open the door for worries. It usually starts with one negative thought, which leads to another, which leads to another, until suddenly you feel overwhelmed. A person lying in bed half awake is stuck in no-man's land. Jumping out of bed and getting into your morning routine quickly gets your day off on the right foot and helps keep negative thoughts at bay.

To avoid the twilight zone at night, don't go to bed until you're tired physically. Being only tired emotionally or mentally may cause you to toss and turn for hours, while being tired physically helps you fall asleep quickly. Engaging in physical exercise during the day can help, but it is important to exercise before 7:00 p.m. (Exercising after that stimulates you when you should be winding down and may interfere with your sleep pattern.) Soaking in a hot tub, reading a good book, or listening to calm music before bedtime can also help you get drowsy enough to fall asleep quickly.

As the classic TV series showed us, the twilight zone can be a strange and frightening place. It's best to avoid it.

UMBRELLA

It was a warm, rainy morning, and Wendy walked down the street glad that her umbrella was keeping her dry. But she was a little bored and, just for fun, she decided to hold the umbrella upside down to collect rain water. It filled to almost overflowing, and a few curious people stopped to see what she was doing. Soon it was too heavy for her to hold steady and water spilled out, splashing onto her and the bystanders. With soaked pant legs, shoes, and socks, they were each cold and wet for the rest of the day. Some of them even got sick with colds and flu afterwards.

APPLICATION

Anger, bitterness, unforgiveness

EXPLANATION

Oftentimes when someone says something that hurts your feelings, instead of getting mad, you tell yourself to let it go. However, throughout the day, you remember the hurtful words. You mull the conversation over and over and think about it before dozing off to sleep. During the week, the words continue to haunt you, and your hurt feelings turn to anger then to bitterness. Before you know it, you are telling your friends about it. Of course, they agree with you because they want to be supportive, but the more you talk about it, the angrier you become. Those whom you tell also become upset with the one who hurt you.

By holding a grudge against your friend, you may think you're in control of the situation; however, she is unaware of the negative feelings you are having, and she is getting on with her life. All the while, you are the only one who is miserable.

An unforgiving person tries to put the offender in an emotional prison by holding a grudge. The irony is that the anger and bitterness actually imprisons only the one who holds the grudge. Many times nurturing negative emotions can cause a person to become physically ill because physical health is directly related to emotional health.

Everything about an umbrella is designed to keep a person dry. It is made of waterproof fabric so the water can't soak through, and the shape of the umbrella funnels rain around you so you will not get wet.

When God made you, He put emotions in your heart so you can experience all types of feelings. He knew that sometimes you would get mad and that long-term anger could damage you. In the Bible, He teaches us to forgive others when they hurt us. Forgiveness is for your benefit. By letting go of ill feelings, you are able to experience freedom as you have never experienced it before. Forgiveness is protective, just like an umbrella during a downpour.

Holding on to anger and bitterness is much like holding an umbrella upside down, and after a while, the bad feelings begin to spill out all over the place, affecting everyone around you. Like walking around all day with wet shoes and socks makes your feet get cold and causes you to be more susceptible to a virus, unforgiveness can cause you to get sick, too.

Gossiping about the problem worsens the relationship between you and your friend because people often end up trashing the one who caused the pain, which may give you a false sense of satisfaction. Eventually, though, the hurt and bitterness return with a vengeance, and the bad feelings spread like wildfire, invading other parts of your life as well. You may find yourself becoming frequently angry at situations and people for no reason.

If you have a problem with someone, swallow your fear and pride and go talk to the person directly. The person may not have said anything to hurt you intentionally and the whole thing could be a simple misunderstanding.

Clearing the air with your friend will deepen your relationship immensely.

Take Daisy for instance. One day while she and a fellow parishioner were working together in the church kitchen, the woman became a bit bossy with Daisy. Instead of letting those feelings get to her, Daisy talked openly with the woman about it and asked if there was a problem. It seems that the woman did not mean to be bossy toward Daisy, but it was her nature to do so, and she apologized. Since getting this out in the open, Daisy and the woman have become much closer and they understand each other better.

You see, a friend is not a friend until you are able to share each other's pain. When that happens, you set yourself free from an emotional prison.

There are other times, though, when you will not be able to connect with your offender. Perhaps he moved away or maybe he died. In those cases, it is important for you to really let go of the hurt. Think of an excuse for what the person said or did. Maybe he had a bad day and took it out on you unintentionally.

The choice to let go is yours alone to make. No one can do that for you. But remember, unforgiveness affects your ability to function mentally, emotionally, physically and even spiritually.

"And when you stand praying, if you hold anything against anyone, forgive them, so that your Father in heaven may forgive you your sins." (Mark 11:25)

Give the injustice to God and let Him take care of it.

". . . whoever touches you touches the apple of his eye—I will surely raise my hand against them so that their slaves will plunder them" (Zechariah 2:8b–9a).

Do you trust God to protect you? Do you trust that God loves you that much?

When Angelina was mistreated by a woman at work, she decided to let God take care of the injustice. There years later, the woman was dismissed from the company. She chose to trust God patiently for three years. God took care of her injustice.

If someone hurts you, do you want to hold the umbrella right side up and let the hurt slide off (trust God), or do you want to hold the umbrella upside down to soak in the hurt and spill over yourself and everyone around you (unforgiveness)? It is up to you to decide. The sooner you can let go, the sooner you will be free.

WHAT ABOUT BOB?

In the movie, *What About Bob?*, Bob (played by Bill Murray) went through life telling himself, "If I meet someone who I don't think likes me, I tell myself, 'Bob, this (the phone) is just temporarily out of order. You know, don't break the connection, just hang up and try again.'"

Living out that philosophy caused others to resent him because he continued to disrespect their boundaries; nonetheless, it kept him from giving up trying to connect with them. Because of his persistency, he earned the affection of his therapist's family members even though his therapist (played by Richard Dreyfuss) hated him.

APPLICATION

Loneliness

EXPLANATION

Having a sense of belonging is one of our basic human needs. Children feel sad and rejected when there is no one with whom to play at school, teens feel rejected when they are not included in social activities, people feel lonely when they have no friends, and older people feel frightened when they have no one to call if they need help.

It is normal to feel rejection sometimes, but there are those who feel it all the time, and that is not normal. A person who always feels rejected has convinced himself that he is unlovable based on past rejection experiences. Without close family ties or friendship bonds, he could easily slip into depression as he imagines co-workers or family members getting together and purposely excluding him. Soon he could spiral into a deeper depression as he becomes consumed with the lie that he is unlovable.

Other negative thoughts could include wanting to be more like someone else, believing success would come by being taller, shorter, more masculine or feminine, smarter, richer, or having a different job or family. There is no end to the destructive lies that can enter one's thinking. Left unchecked, a person could believe suicide is a better alternative than living and that others would then be sorry and maybe even miss him.

Annie, a fifteen-year-old teenager, had a difficult time fitting in. In her church youth group, she felt ignored by her peers and couldn't help but notice the faces that were made when she spoke up. Desperately wanting to be accepted, she continued taking chances and trying to buddy up, but to no avail. In her heart she felt sad, rejected, and very, very alone. It was the same at school, too, and she really didn't understand what she was doing wrong. Whether she tried to be funny, serious, or nonchalant, it seemed that kids her age simply were not interested in what she had to say or what she wanted to do.

On Mondays in the cafeteria, she would listen to the girls talk about their weekend and how much fun they'd had. They gossiped about who was dating whom, which couple was breaking up, or the horrid outfit so-and-so was wearing.

Annie's heart was breaking, and no one seemed to know or care. *If only I was dead*, she thought to herself, *maybe somebody would care.*

When she moved away from the group and ate alone at lunchtime, no one even noticed. This made the pain worse as Annie realized how alone she really was.

She began cutting herself, but that only relieved the pain for a while. After a failed suicide attempt, she sought help from Dr. Rita.

It took several visits before Annie trusted the counselor enough to tell about the hurts in her heart. Tears rolled down her face session after session until the pain subsided and she could begin talking. Today Annie is a confident young lady who is gifted in singing, and she no longer obsesses about whether or not others like her.

Annie had to accept the fact that she was not an outgoing person. Being an introvert meant that she was not one to start up a conversation or be the center of attention. Rather, she was more comfortable doing things with one friend at a time. She also had to accept that others could not read her mind, and if she wanted to have friends, she would have to do some work. Dr. Rita suggested that Annie make a list of people with whom she'd like to be friends and would feel comfortable calling on the phone.

When Annie felt like going shopping or to a movie, she mustered the inner strength to call someone on the list. Like Bob (in *What About Bob?*), Annie made up excuses for anyone unable to go with her, and that way she didn't let her feelings get hurt.

One time she called Suzie to go out, but Suzie said she couldn't go because she already had plans. Instead of taking it personally and getting her feelings hurt, Annie told herself, *I know she's busy with sports today. We'll just go out another time.* This allowed her to shrug it off and simply pick up the phone and call someone else.

She also decided to expand her circle of friends to include those of different age groups. Elderly folks had lots of wisdom and experience from which she could draw, and youngsters provided amusement and silly playtime that she enjoyed. Annie was surprised to discover that she liked doing things with other people, regardless of their age.

Dr. Rita also suggested that she make a list of things to do when she was alone. Annie's list grew quite lengthy, and she posted it on her bedroom wall. She wrote down things such as organizing and cleaning her bedroom, going for walks, swimming, biking, drawing, painting, cooking, doing a good deed, and making a craft. Whenever she was bored or wanted to be alone, she would pick one of the items and enjoy her time doing that.

Along with her expanding list of things she enjoyed, she discovered that she had a beautiful singing voice. She began taking singing lessons, which helped release stress and build her self-confidence. Not only did she like the sound of her own voice but she realized that she was beginning not to care what others thought about her.

She tried out for the school choir and a school play, and was accepted into both. She volunteered to help children learn to read, which gave her life a purpose deeper than self-enjoyment. At church, she joined a small weekly Bible study group with people her own age. The group became quite close as they studied and shared their lives with one another.

Annie was now in control of her life. She had several friends with whom she went out on a regular basis, and as she met more people, she added them to her list. During lunch hour, she no longer tried to fit in with the popular group but instead she occupied her time talking with one friend or reading a novel.

Before, she dreaded being alone because it meant that she had no friends. But now when she was alone, it was because she chose to be. She learned that Jesus even needed to have time alone, and knowing that helped her relax and enjoy herself.

Annie no longer had the time or desire to entertain negative thoughts, gossip, or drama. In her busy life, she was now accomplishing much more than she had ever before dreamed possible. For the first time in her young life, she was very happy.

By becoming friends with herself, she had become a friend to everyone.

RELATIONSHIPS

THE BAND-AID RELATIONSHIP

John was running late for work and was hurrying to make his lunch. In his haste, he cut his finger with a sharp knife.

"Ouch!"

He dropped the knife, grabbed a paper napkin, and pressed the cut to stop the bleeding. He hurried to find the antibiotic cream and a Band-Aid. Now he was going to be even later, and he was thoroughly aggravated with himself.

To calm himself down, he took a deep breath and told himself to relax.

The rest of the day was uneventful, but every time he used that finger, the pain and the bulky bandage reminded him of his impatience earlier that morning.

By the end of the day, John had become accustomed to both the Band-Aid and the hurting finger, even though both were inconvenient. After showering that night, he saw that the cut was still red and swollen and decided to keep it covered for a few more days.

John paid little attention to it after that, and the cut began to heal. The bandage didn't bother him anymore, and instead of seeming inconvenient, he grew accustomed to the bulk, almost as though it was an extension of his own skin.

After a week or so, there was no longer any need for the bandage, so John peeled it off and threw it away.

The band-aid, which had served its purpose of protecting the wound from the elements, was not needed anymore. It was now utterly useless.

APPLICATION

Broken relationships

EXPLANATION

Susan had been in an exclusive relationship with Steven for about a year. They had talked about marriage and someday raising a family of their own.

But that was not to be, and one day Steven coldly announced that their relationship was over and that he wanted to date other women.

Susan didn't see this coming and was crushed. She felt as though her whole world had collapsed. How could he betray her like this? As hard as she tried to snap out of it, all she could feel was pain from the rejection.

Memories of their time together haunted her. The scent of a man's cologne transported her to another time and place with Steven. When she caught sight of a man with red hair, she was reminded of his red hair, and the pain would start all over again.

Her emotions were like a roller coaster. One day she would feel up, thinking things were getting better, and then suddenly loneliness or anger would send her plummeting to the depths. She feared that she might be alone forever and never have a family of her own.

Then she met James. He was nice looking, rather quiet, and had a nice job. They dated a few times, and it soon became apparent that he wanted everything she wanted: a family, a nice home, and long walks on the beach. Although Susan didn't love him, she felt safe with him and unafraid. Their relationship progressed quickly, more so than she really wanted.

It felt good to have someone at her beck and call. The flowers, the phone calls, and the surprise late-night visits were a welcome relief from the blackness she had experienced for so long. On the flip side, however, James didn't seem to have other friends to hang out with, nor did he have outside interests.

James began talking about marriage and was almost insistent that they not wait very long. But Susan was uneasy. Because she hadn't taken time to examine the relationship, she was unable to put her finger on what was wrong and what she was really feeling. She began to pull away from James, and explained that she needed space and time to sort things out. He was hurt and angry. He told her in no uncertain terms that because he had given everything to her, he expected the same commitment from her.

Susan gave in that time, but the tension in her heart did not subside. Soon she was thoroughly tired of the constant struggle and finally gathered the strength she needed to call it quits.

What really happened in this relationship? What was really going on?

James was a rescuer, a protector, a caretaker, who was attracted to Susan because she was in pain. He saw himself as her knight in shining armor.

In short, James was Susan's "Band-Aid."

To him it seemed a perfect match. And it felt that way to Susan, too . . . for a short time.

Protecting her gave James a sense of empowerment and satisfaction. He wrapped himself tightly around Susan's broken heart.

This new relationship provided a fresh start for Susan, or so it seemed. Instead of being lonely, she now had an almost constant companion. Because the relationship was built on a rescue/rescued basis, it soon stifled and smothered Susan. It was unhealthy from the get-go.

While she was being shielded from further pain, her heart was also on the mend.

As she began to heal, her need for a Band-Aid became less and less. It was inevitable for Susan to peel herself away from James' overbearing presence and stand once more on her own two feet.

Why was James a rescuer? Why would anyone want to be a rescuer? People who take that role often do not consciously realize that they have, and they will inevitably find themselves discarded and hurt. If not careful, a rescuer can spend his or her entire lifetime being a Band-Aid for others and end up hurt every time.

Throughout life, do you find yourself being the wounded one? Are you the rescuer, the Band-Aid?

Examine your relationships. If you discover that you have a pattern of hurting others or of being hurt, seek professional help to find out why. End this destructive pattern so your wounded heart can heal. You do not have to continue making the same disastrous relational mistakes again and again. There is hope and healing for you!

CELL PHONE

The cell phone has been the most important invention in the recent years. One day without the cell phone will devastate many individuals. They talk on it, text or email with it, find all kinds of information on it. Whenever you need to talk, whether it is a serious, casual, or business conversation, the cell phone is always there at your service.

Sometimes your friends, relatives, and business associates might be so busy that they are unable to answer your phone calls. But you can always text or email a message to them, and they can respond at their convenience. If you need to locate some information, whether it is finding a pair of shoes or locating research documents, the Web is at your service on your cell phone any time you need it. Additionally, your cell phone can give you directions to reach your destination. If you have an emergency on the road, you can always rely on your cell phone to allow you to call for help.

When your cell phone is at your service every minute of the day, you take it for granted. You feel so lost when you must go without it for only one day. Do you have the same feeling when you don't have the Bible with you? Do you feel lost when you don't communicate with God? Do you spend more time on the phone than with the Lord?

APPLICATION

Relationships

EXPLANATION

When Henry first gets up in the morning, he checks his schedule on his cell phone, then he starts making phone calls to his customers before he even connects with his wife. He grabs some breakfast and is ready to be on the road. He talks on the phone while driving to work. Of course, he will be on his cell phone all day long at work. He uses his cell phone to find directions to get to a business meeting. While he is at lunch, he returns text messages. After lunch, he continues to be on his cell phone for the rest of the afternoon. As soon as he gets in the car to drive home, his phone rings again. He talks to his wife for a few minutes and then has to excuse himself to answer a conference call with a customer. He finally gets home. His wife and his kids want to talk to him, but he is too busy talking on the phone. They all go out to eat, but Henry continues to talk on the phone while he is eating.

His wife plans a family vacation so that they can be together to connect. Henry, of course, brings his Blackberry so he can talk or check his email or text messages. His wife and kids have no chance to get his attention. It seems that every vacation follows the same pattern.

Henry's wife is feeling very lonely in their marriage. It is all right for the moment because she devotes all her time and energy to the kids. As long as she has the kids to occupy herself, she is able to tolerate not being able to connect with Henry.

Years go by, and as the last child finally leaves home, Henry's wife becomes so depressed that she uses alcohol to numb her emotional pain. Even when she and Henry have opportunities to talk, neither of them has an idea of what to talk about. They are like strangers to each other. Henry's wife continues to get more depressed each day, and the alcohol only worsens her depression. She begs her husband to talk to her and to go for counseling, but Henry is too busy to listen to his wife's suggestion. He thinks there is nothing wrong with the marriage. His conclusion is that his wife just has a hard time adjusting to not having kids at home.

One day, Henry goes to work as usual, and he continues to connect with the cell phone as usual. When he comes home after work, he finds a note on the kitchen counter from his wife indicating that she is leaving home for good, and she will not continue to be his wife. A month later, he receives the divorce papers. He tries to find his wife, but she is nowhere to be found.

With no one to turn to, Henry decides to go to church to seek God. He asks for God's forgiveness. He wants to let God take control of his life. God's Word touches Henry's soul and encourages and empowers him. He finds that he wants to read God's Word as often as he can. God's Word comes alive to him as God gives him the verses he needs at the right time. He begins to spend more time in the Bible than on the cell phone.

Overuse of the cell phone damages relationships. Overuse of the Bible builds relationship with God and people. Hence, Henry carries his Bible all day long, knowing that when God's love is in him, his love will leak out to other people around him. Henry can now love people the way God loves them—unconditionally. Whenever he needs direction, he reads God's Word. Whenever he feels alone, he finds verses in the Bible to give him assurance that he is not alone and that God will never forsake him. When he feels discouraged, he calls a Christian friend to pray with him. His friend usually gives him some Bible verses to memorize. When Henry recites the Bible verses, he usually feels better.

As he looks back to his marriage, Henry remembers how his wife used to complain about his talking on his cell phone so much that she and their kids had no chance to connect with him. He lost so many years that could have been so precious to him. He wishes he would have listened to his wife and gotten help for their marriage. He wishes he would have turned off the cell phone when he came home or was on vacation with the family. Now there is no way to repair it. He misses his wife deeply, and his kids have no contact with him. Since he did not spend time with them, he is a stranger to them. They don't even miss him. It really does not matter if he is successful in his career anymore. He wants to start over again with his wife and kids, but it is too late.

Henry continues to live his life as a single person who loves God. He no longer carries his cell phone all day long; instead, he carries his Bible with him wherever he goes. He is so close to God that he wants to communicate with Him every moment of the day. He treasures his Bible, and he often buys extra ones to give away as gifts. He tries to live a God-honoring life for he knows God has forgiven all of his sins, including failing to be a loving husband.

One afternoon while he was eating lunch in a restaurant, Henry saw his wife for the first time since they were divorced four years earlier. They sat together and talked for hours. He asked his wife to forgive him for everything he had done to her and the kids. He admitted that he had spent too much time on his cell phone and had neglected her and the kids. He had been living under this guilt for years. His wife told him that she had remarried and divorced after one year. She asked him if they could start dating again. One year later, they remarried. His wife accepted Christ while they were dating again. Now Henry knows that God is giving him a second chance.

Henry is very attentive to his wife. He calls her many times throughout the day to connect with her. When he comes home from work, he shuts off the cell phone and concentrates on his wife. They read the Bible and pray together every night. They are always doing fun things together. When they go on trips, Henry no longer takes his Blackberry so that he and his wife can focus on each other. Instead, they bring their black leather Bible so they can read it together before going to bed. Henry has never experienced so much joy in his life.

Investing your time in people will give you meaning in life. Spending time acquiring material things of this world will give you temporary satisfaction, but eventually you will lose the most important things in life—people. Keeping a balance between work and people you love is the most essential ingredient that will give you joy and satisfaction.

The cell phone was designed to improve your life in many ways, but if you overuse it, it can destroy your relationships with people, especially your loved ones. Take control of your cell phone before it controls you! Invest time in the Bible and in your relationship with God and your family. After all, they are the ones that give unconditional love. They will be there whenever you need them.

FROZEN OR MELTING MOMENTS

Mary had trouble with relationships. When a friend, relative, or coworker showed any sign of negative emotion, such as raising her voice, making an angry facial expression, or saying a confrontational statement, Mary would freeze up, get tongue-tied, and break out in a sweat. The thought of someone getting the least bit upset with her made her sick to her stomach and tremble with fear. She told herself it was childish to behave this way, but no amount of self-discipline resulted in change. So to keep from rocking the boat, she would not say anything at all and simply pretend everything was just fine.

Life is not always fine, however, and there are times when everyone needs to admit that a problem exists and then buckle down to work out a solution. When a person refuses to admit there are problems, that is called denial, and when situations are left to fester and grow, over time they build up like water behind a dam, and eventually it will all come gushing out.

Because of her insecurities, Mary could not deal with relational issues in a rational manner, and even though she pretended they were not there, she still could not forget about them. Instead, she would stew day and night about something someone had said, or a "look" someone had given her. As a result, her stomach was in knots most of the time, and she developed irritable bowel syndrome.

While Mary was desperate for friendships and longed to be loved, the idea was also frightening. How could she get close to someone without getting her feelings hurt? How could she ever handle negative emotions? Mary never saw her parents have a healthy disagreement; therefore, she concluded that all disagreements were ugly fights, which had to end on a destructive note. To her, that was simply too risky to chance, so she opted to stay alone. As a result, she was miserable and often cried herself to sleep at night. When someone did pay attention to her, she would melt and go overboard to keep that person's friendship. However, as soon as the new friend exhibited a negative emotion, Mary would freeze up and turn inward, trying to protect herself.

At one time, Mary had been in a relationship with a guy she thought she loved, but it turned abusive. She was so afraid of hurting his feelings or disappointing him that she could not make even the simplest of choices, such as deciding what restaurant to dine in or what movie to see. Every time he asked her what she wanted to do, she would not give an answer. Over time, his frustration escalated, and he became more and more aggressive, to the point that he was pushing her and eventually began hitting her. She finally clammed up altogether, and one day he said he'd had enough and told her to get lost. It was a lose-lose situation—one she did not care to repeat. Embarrassed that she was being used as a punching bag, she shut herself off from her family and confided in no one about what was happening. She was a nervous wreck and didn't trust anyone, including herself.

What was wrong with Mary? She had a heart of gold, would do anything for anyone, and was one of the most giving people in her office, yet remained the loneliest of all. If only she knew how to relate to people without getting hurt.

APPLICATION

Relationships

EXPLANATION

Mary finally got fed up with always having hurt feelings and always being afraid and lonely. One day she decided to get help from Christian counselor, Dr. Rita. In sessions, Mary made several self-discoveries and learned why she acted and reacted in ways that were harmful. She also learned what the Bible had to say about who she was in Christ. Dr. Rita gently encouraged her as she struggled to recall the childhood torment she had endured. From a therapist's point of view, treatment is sometimes like putting together a puzzle with some of those pieces being difficult to find.

While growing up, Mary's mother was physically and emotionally abusive towards her. When she became angry, her face would tighten; she would squint her eyes and draw her brows. Her lips would form a definite frown and become white from pursing them so tightly. Mary knew then that her mother was going to start hitting her and she would brace herself for the beating that would leave her bruised and gasping for air. As if the beatings weren't enough, Mary's mother would often tell her what a disappointing child she was and how she would probably not amount to anything.

Unable to protect herself, Mary was also sexually abused by a few guys as a young teen. She certainly was not safe telling her mother, and there was no other adult in her life to whom she could go, so she bore that shame and humiliation as well. Mary considered herself an object of little worth.

Dr. Rita assured Mary that her reaction to unpleasant situations was normal, considering her background, and explained the importance of learning how to react positively to everyday strife. She explained about healthy boundaries and the need for them in her life.

Slowly Mary began walking the road to recovery. With Dr. Rita's assistance, she learned how and when to speak up for herself. She accepted that it is normal for every relationship to have moments of tension and learned how to work through them without screaming or silently retreating. Working through any program of healing can be tough, and there were times when Mary felt like throwing in the towel. On those days, she would step back and look at the progress she'd made and look at where she wanted to go, and then make the decision to press on.

Mary's demeanor began to change as her confidence grew. Not only was she starting to relate to others in healthy ways, but she was also beginning a new relationship with her Heavenly Father. She learned that because God is the one and only true King, she is a Princess in His Kingdom. She asked why such a loving God would allow her to be hurt. To her amazement, she found that it is never God's will for anyone to be hurt, but because He gave all people a free will, sometimes they make horrible choices which affect others, like Mary, in very bad ways. The good news is that God always provides help and healing from the injuries received on life's journey.

For the first time in her life, Mary began extending herself in friendships. Sure, there were times when she was afraid and times when she regressed, but she continued implementing her newly found life skills. Before long, she was included in outings and get-togethers with other women her age. Not only was she beginning to trust them, but they were beginning to trust her, and sometimes Mary could not contain her tears of joy and thankfulness.

If you have experienced situations similar to Mary's and have trouble reacting in positive ways, do not lose heart because help is available for you. The Lord is waiting for you to come to Him. He has many gifts for you, and one of them is peace.

In John 14:27 (in the New Testament of the Bible), Jesus said, "I am leaving you with a gift—peace of mind and heart. And the peace I give isn't like the peace the world gives. So don't be troubled or afraid."

THE HIPPO THAT FELL OFF THE SEESAW

Hippo and Elle have been sitting on opposite ends of a see-saw for quite some time. Hippo wants it to go up and down like it's supposed to, but Elle doesn't push. She only sits there. Over and over Hippo pushes with his powerful legs, but usually the most he can get is to make the see-saw balance midway off the ground.

Sometimes he gets very frustrated and pushes hard, sending Elle's side down, but because she doesn't push her side, the see-saw is soon balancing again. Hippo doesn't know what to do. He yells at her, encourages her, and even blames her, but nothing changes. She simply refuses to cooperate. He wonders if she is deaf, or if she doesn't love him, or what is the problem. He could get off the see-saw and walk away, but he loves Elle and doesn't want to see-saw with anyone else.

Once more he gives another push with his powerful legs, sending Elle's end all the way down to the ground. And then she does something she hasn't done in a long time. She gives a gentle push and slowly, slowly, her end goes up and Hippo's end goes down. Hippo looks at Elle's face. She doesn't really know what to do. She looks surprised and maybe a little scared.

And then Elle starts to slide down the see-saw toward Hippo. Down, down, down she goes until . . . PLOP! She lands right on top of him! Then Hippo and Elle laugh and laugh because it turned out to be so much fun.

APPLICATION

Husband-wife relationships; parent-child relationships

EXPLANATION

When a couple is having problems in their relationship, one of the partners often complains that he or she is the only one that is doing all the "work" to keep things going smoothly. When one does a good deed, that person wants a favor in return. He is willing to give, but expects to get back and complains when he doesn't, much the same as Hippo in the above story. The result is negative, and both partners end up feeling miserable.

Unless one is willing to give sacrificially, without expecting anything in return, the battle goes on, sometimes for years. But when one gives without expecting anything back, the relationship will slowly start to heal and move forward. Hopefully, one day the receiving partner will respond to the giving partner's love and attention. When both partners exercise a giving attitude, with no expectation from the other, the relationship begins to grow, and over time, will grow deeper and become a "safe place."

The same principle applies to the emotional closeness between parents and their children. For example, a mother whose aspirations for her son are unrealistic may withhold affection until she approves of his behavior or until he achieves the outcome she desires. This causes the child to grow up feeling insecure and depressed. By the time that child reaches the teenage years, he has learned that his mother's acceptance is conditional and based on performance. This creates a huge gap not only in the parent-child relationship, but also in the child's emotional growth.

Unrealistic parental expectations come from a number of things. When a mother wants to prove to the world that her children are the brightest, she will expect her children to always be on the honor roll. When a father wants his son to be the best in sports, he will expect him to be the star of the team. When a parent didn't achieve recognition while growing up and wants to live vicariously through his or her child, that parent can place unrealistic expectations on the child. These aspects and more all play into how parents interact with their children in a negative way. Now let's look at the positive.

A son whose mother loves him unconditionally, without expecting anything in return, *even when he misbehaves or fails,* will grow up feeling safe and secure. The mother provides safe and healthy boundaries for the relationship. As the son grows and matures, he will undoubtedly share some of his feelings and thoughts openly with her, knowing that her love for him is true, deep, and non-judgmental. A father who encourages his children to play in sports but does not demand perfection creates a healthy, competitive spirit in them and teaches them that it is okay to play and have fun, whether they win or lose.

The security developed in this type of relationship creates a close bond that will last a lifetime and, more than likely, span several generations.

HOLES IN THE BUCKET

Jon looked with disgust at the silver bucket he had just filled with water.

Its silver color was unique, with the underlying tones of blue. The emblem imprinted on the bottom told the story of where the bucket was made. Although it was purchased with practical purposes in mind, the bucket had sentimental value because he had found it while vacationing overseas. A special hook near the rear door entrance was made especially for the bucket so that visitors could see his treasure whenever they entered his house.

To his disappointment, however, the bucket would not hold water for any length of time. Every time he used this bucket, he would start out feeling excited because he was going to get some of work done. But usually he ended up frustrated because the water seemed to simply evaporate! Frequently he had to return to the faucet for a refill.

With each use, Jon's frustration level rose because he was never able to complete his projects in a timely manner. One day he became so angry that he kicked the bucket into the side of an outbuilding and it landed upside down. When he picked it up, he noticed a very small hole on the bottom side, next to the emblem. Over the next several days he tried to repair the hole, but nothing seemed to work. Finally he pitched it high into the air and when it came crashing down, it hit a rock, causing the sides to bend. The mangled, worthless bucket had caused him enough grief, and Jon decided to throw it away.

To his surprise, having it gone was such a big relief that he didn't even miss it!

APPLICATION

Relationships

EXPLANATION

The bucket in this story represents someone who is emotionally needy, such as Jon's girlfriend, Teresa.

When Jon gives Teresa attention or help, she is never satisfied and always wants more. She expects him to be the only person in the world to fill her love tank. In the beginning, Teresa would ask Jon to help her to fix things at her house. Gradually, she started asking his advice and then she began expecting him to solve her problems. When Jon gave her suggestions, she would not agree with him; but neither could she come up with a better answer. She would ask him to help her make decisions, but if things did not turn out the way she wanted, she would blame him. First, she demanded him to fix material things, then she expected him to fix her circumstances, and eventually she expected him to fix and meet her emotional needs.

Teresa unrealistically expected Jon to be at her beck and call any time of the day or night. Several times a day she would call, and if he didn't answer, she would hang up and call back repeatedly until he did answer, and then she would scream at him for not being available. She blamed him for her grief, for her anger, and for her fears. She wanted and expected Jon to be by her side every single minute of the day, but even when he was, she still wasn't happy.

Jon could not make Teresa happy. No one could. You see, happiness comes from the inside. Teresa's emotions were hers to choose, and Jon could not make her feel one way or the other about anything.

Teresa came from a home where she had no emotional connection with her father, who was critical and verbally abusive towards her. She remembered him pushing her away as she clung to his legs for comfort when she was only three. She could not remember him kissing or hugging her. Not ever. Not even one time. How she wished she could have sat on his lap. She hated him and loved him intensely at the same time. The emotional void in her heart left her with the false notion that she had no feelings and no needs.

"I can take care of myself; I don't need anyone," she told herself over and over while growing up.

In adulthood, she felt entitled to be loved and cared for and so demanded it from those around her. Her neediness was like that leaky bucket, which could never be filled up. And she especially craved for a man's attention.

Once she latched onto a man, she could not let go. If the guy left her, she would be so depressed and so filled with anxiety that it seemed her world had collapsed. Through counseling, she worked on her "father wound" by grieving over that childhood loss. After many years of separation from him, they reconnected. She learned that he had mellowed and had even gone through counseling. He apologized for the pain he had caused, and today they have a decent relationship.

Healing from her father wound has caused her to enjoy healthier relationships with other men, and more importantly, with God.

Jon, on the other hand, represented someone who was a rescuer. He felt compelled to help a woman close to him who had great emotional needs. He would start by doing one good deed and then would feel guilty for not saving her from anger or sadness, or whatever negative situation would come to light. In the end, he wound up being a slave, trapped in a relationship with seemingly no way out. No matter how much he gave, it was never enough. Like trying to fill a bucket with a hole on the bottom, Jon never had enough to fill it up. Never enough love. Never enough time. Never enough money. There simply was never enough.

When Jon was very young, his father left his mother for another woman and Jon became his mother's caretaker. Truthfully, he was almost like a substitute husband for her. When his mother was sad, he would comfort her. When she was mad, he would stop whatever he was doing to help her calm down. He even taught himself how to be handy around the house. As an adult, the caretaker role continued.

Jon's compulsion to rescue took its toll on his career and friendships. Through counseling he was able to connect his past and present struggles rationally, as well as experience the pain in his childhood emotionally. Eventually, Jon understood the need to sever the unhealthy relationship with Teresa and get his life together. He thought it would be a devastating thing to do, but instead he found that having it over and done with was quite a relief.

In the same way that Jon was happier after ridding himself of that faulty bucket, he also realized he needed to heal emotionally before having close, intimate relationships. He learned how to set boundaries and improved his assertiveness skills. Most importantly, his relationship with God improved, and the Lord helped him in the area of setting necessary boundaries. The more he healed, the more in control of his life he became, and the healthier was his outlook.

MR. GREEN SQUARE AND MISS GREEN CIRCLE

Mr. Green Square had lots of friends. Some were shaped like circles, others like squares, and still others were shaped like triangles.

The Hippo That Fell Off the Seesaw

Whenever there was free time, they'd all hang out together, swapping stories and telling jokes, which they found hilariously funny. They'd laugh and laugh until they got cramps in their stomachs.

One day when they were at a park, Mr. Green Square saw Miss Green Circle, an attractive gal who was new to the group. He walked over and introduced himself. A magical feeling immediately connected the two. Sparks flew, and it almost felt like electricity.

Truly, he thought to himself, *this must indeed be love at first sight.*

Later that night after Mr. Green Square had gone home, he had a hard time getting to sleep because he could not get Miss Green Circle out of his mind. Even when he closed his eyes, it seemed as though she was there before him. Several nights passed, and finally he could stand it no longer. He picked up the phone and gave Miss Green Circle a call and asked if she would go out with him. She accepted, and thus began their dating journey.

Every day they talked on the phone, listening intently to each other's stories. They loved hearing about each other's past, finding out how the other's day went at work, and learning about each other's dreams for the future.

Of course, they realized they were different shapes, but that didn't bother them. Their interest in each other was so intense that their shapes were simply not an issue. They were in love, and as far as they were concerned, that's all that mattered.

After about a year, Mr. Green Square asked Miss Green Circle to marry him, and without hesitation, she said yes. They could hardly wait for the big day to arrive. Miss Green Circle wasted no time in beginning wedding preparations.

After they were married, however, things began to change. Miss Green Circle started telling her husband how he should act and what he should say. She expected him to act like a circle, not a square, and to fit in with her family. Likewise, Mr. Green Square expected his wife to behave as though she was square. After all, how did she expect to ever fit in with his family if she continued to behave like a circle?

Is it really possible for a person to change into something he or she is not? Were the expectations of this couple realistic or unrealistic?

APPLICATION
Relationships

EXPLANATION

In real life, it is often the case that couples blindly accept each other's differences before marriage. They somehow view their differences as virtues rather than flaws. By looking through "rose-colored glasses," they allow themselves to see only the good in each other. When flaws become apparent, each somehow makes excuses for the other because of their strong feelings. After marriage, when reality sets in, they begin to see each other as they really are.

The differences really come to light once a child is born into the marriage relationship. Because each parent was raised in a particular manner, completely apart from the other, the differences can be very strong and emotions can erupt. Instead of accepting the differences, each parent attempts to change the other so they will be more alike. The husband may think, "If only my wife would change, everything would be okay." The wife thinks, "He is the one with a problem. If only he would change, then our marriage would be good."

If they go to see a counselor, the husband might try to persuade the counselor his wife is supposed to act or think because that was how his family acted and thought. A couple in this situation can easily get caught in this battle, with neither one wanting to give up the idea of "fixing" the other person.

The following is a real-life example of a couple trapped in this kind of battle.

Jim was brought up in a home where his mother was a stay-at-home mom. She kept the house sparkling clean. Never was there dust on any counter or table top. When he married Nina, he expected her to keep the house as clean as his mother did. That, however, was an unrealistic expectation, and she did not live up to it. Instead, Nina divided her time between working full time and caring for the family after work.

When Nina was growing up, both of her parents worked, so everyone pitched in and did chores, including her dad. After she got married, she fully expected Jim to help around the house. Contrary to her wishes, however, he complained about how messy the house was and never gave her any help.

Worst of all, Jim continued to confront Nina and ruin her spirit. When he tried to hug her, she would pull away from him because she simply could not hug an alligator. Jim, on the other hand, felt rejected and unloved when Nina refused to hug or have sexual intimacy with him. They both thought if the other person would change, their marriage would be restored.

During counseling sessions, Jim and Nina kept attacking each other and brought out each other's flaws. The battle raged on as they continued to blame each other, rather than to accept their own portion of responsibility. The truth of the matter was that it was just as impossible for Jim to turn into Nina, as it was impossible for Nina to turn into Jim.

Their counselor, Dr. Rita, told them the story of Mr. Green Square and Miss Green Circle. Square has four angles and four sides and a circle has no angles and no sides. As a result, it is impossible for a square to turn into a triangle or a triangle to turn into a square. In order to have a close relationship, they would need to accept each other's differences.

Since they came from totally different family backgrounds, they had to stop thinking that their family of origin's way of handling things was the only way. They needed to try to understand the differences between the two families and come up with their own way of handling things—a way that would work for their own family.

It was important for Jim and Nina to learn that differences are neither right nor wrong; they are only differences. Dr. Rita was able to point out to them that it wasn't their differences that were the problem; rather, it was their insistence on getting their own way, which almost destroyed their marriage and family.

The couple also had different personality types. To help them discover their own uniqueness, they took personality tests. They discovered that not only did they have many differences, but they also had many similarities. Dr. Rita showed them ways of accepting each other's differences rather than trying to change each other. Focusing on changes they each could make, as well as giving and taking, was another vital ingredient to their success. After all, no matter how much Jim or Nina wanted to change each other, they would never be able to. Even if they had tried to change for the other person, it would never have worked. A circle cannot change into a square and vice versa.

God makes everyone unique for a reason. To be compatible with others, experiment with various options that might work, and be flexible in the process. For example, take the parents who are considering whether to send their child to a public school or a private school. The analytical parent may look at the cost of the private school and be more concerned with the financial aspect; whereas, the feeling parent will consider how it may feel to the child to attend a large public school. Putting their ideas together will help them come up with the best solution because they will have covered all angles of the problem.

God purposely made you and me different from anyone else in the whole world. And those very differences are what He will use to complement your relationships. God carefully and lovingly intended to make you different so that you can be the best partner to your spouse, your friends, and your family.

Remember, the only person you can change is yourself. You have no control over changing anyone else, no matter how hard you try!

PAPER PLATE AND CHINA PLATE

When Mary was a little girl, she loved to play house. She had a small table and chairs, and when her friends came over she would set it with pretty dishes and serve cookies and tea. Mary delighted in sharing with her friends and all their little baby dolls.

As she grew, Mary dreamed of having her own home one day and entertaining guests. She thought of how her house would be decorated and how she would set her dining room table with pretty dishes, silverware and napkins. When she was old enough to work, she set aside money from her earnings to save for those special dishes.

She spent time learning how dishes are made, how different types of glass react under varying circumstances, such as how some, when dropped, shatter into a million fragments while others break into larger chunks; some are dishwasher safe and others are not. From this, she was able to decide what type of China she wanted.

Eventually she grew up and married, and the day came when she was ready to purchase her very own dishes. All she had yet to do was to find the perfect pattern.

While out with friends one day, Mary spotted a store specializing in beautiful China, and they all went in to look. They were dazzled by the rows of beautiful glassware, displayed so as to catch the light, which enhanced the colors. Mary was familiar with some of the patterns, but nothing caught her eye right away.

And then she saw it. The most wonderful pattern, and in the exact colors she had chosen for her home's decor. She could hardly believe her eyes! Right there on the spot, Mary purchased a complete set of twelve, with coffee cups, saucers, salad and dinner plates, stemmed glasses, and serving dishes. She was so happy she practically floated home that afternoon.

The dishes were displayed in a China cabinet she had purchased years before, but not only were the pieces beautiful to look at, they were used often when friends or family came over.

The China was gently cared for, washed with special detergents, and dried with super-soft, absorbent cloths. She hand-wiped each piece slowly and carefully every time they were used. To her, the glassware represented the pride she had in her home and the love she had for her family and friends.

Emily

Emily was a happy-go-lucky young woman, fun to be around, and serious only to a point. It seemed that she would go where the wind blew, and she'd get caught up in the moment.

Her parents divorced when she was young, and Emily had to move many times. She had attended several different schools, and she never made long-lasting friendships. She learned not to get too attached to anyone, to show her real feelings, or to get serious. After all, her life changed at the drop of a hat. And even though she was now grown, that carefree lifestyle had become a habit. Because she didn't take the time to stop and give her life real consideration, she did not comprehend what was happening to her—what she was doing to herself.

After graduating from high school, Emily got a job and moved into a small apartment. She bought furniture from here and there, whatever she could afford. Whether or not she liked it was not necessarily a consideration.

Friends were a dime a dozen, and Emily had lots. Her idea of having a good time was to invite her friends over, and their friends, too. Sometimes complete strangers would show up. And while the parties lasted long into the night, she often never saw those strangers again.

Emily was easily bored and went from job to job. Even as an adult, she found herself moving often. Putting down roots was not her lifestyle, and while the thought occurred to her that she might like a home and some long-lasting relationships, maybe even a husband and children, she had no idea how to go about getting life to work that way, and so she never really tried.

Dinnertime for Emily often consisted of a sandwich and something out of a can, eaten from paper plates in front of the TV. She would laugh and say it was easy to do the dishes—just toss and go. "Just like my life," she would say flippantly, "Disposable." But there was a problem with the paper plates. If too much was put on, they would bend, and the contents would dump onto the floor, or if the food was runny it would leak onto her lap, which had happened more times than she could count.

To her, paper plates were representative of her life—temporary, something to use once and then get rid of, easily replaceable, no investment, no effort.

APPLICATION

Adult-teen relationships

EXPLANATION

This story represents two individuals who look at relationships differently.

At first, when Mary spent time waiting for the right partner to come along, she felt lonely and discouraged, especially when her friends had all found their true love. Nonetheless, she waited patiently for Mr. Right to come into her life.

When love came into her life, along with it came some pain, struggles, and difficulties. Nonetheless, Mary patiently cared for her love with nurturing and patience. No relationship is ever without hard times, and Mary's life was no exception. She learned, however, that quiet and careful consideration would often pave the road to health and wholeness in her life. She was in it for better or for worse, and she knew that her partner would need nurturing and room to grow.

Mary read books on how to improve their marriage relationship. She encouraged her husband to go to couples' workshops and retreats. She invested time in having meaningful conversations, and was careful to look out for her husband's best interests. In turn, she taught him what she needed and encouraged him to look out for her best interests as well. They spent time doing fun things together.

At times, they had struggles like everyone does, but they determined ahead of time to work those things out. They did not have the perfect relationship, but they both enjoyed the stability of their relationship.

A relationship, much like the China dishes that Mary so tenderly cared for, also needs TLC. To stay looking new and beautiful, there needs to be thoughtful consideration to eliminate problematic issues. There also needs to be time for play and fun and laughter, as well as soul-searching, tears, and painful honesty.

Emily, on the other hand, represents individuals who do not like to commit to relationships. People who do not take the time to examine their lives often find they are going in circles. Nothing changes, and life becomes painfully routine. Even though a certain degree of change may be desired, it would take extreme measures to do so, and that can be a very scary thing.

It is often painful to look at your background—how you grew up and the things that happened to you. Sometimes we need to admit that our parents, or other people whom we dearly loved, have hurt us deeply. Admitting that can feel as though we are betraying them. But hurting them is not our intent. When we do not examine our lives, we take the risk of continuing to make the same mistakes over and over again. And that is the definition of insanity—doing the same things again and again, but expecting different results.

One dangerous trap in Emily's lifestyle is the "revolving door" love cycle. One day you meet someone and the two of you fall head-over-heels in love. Everything is rosy and sweet. Things move quickly, and sex often comes early in the relationship. But when the feelings begin to taper off, or when they become more even-keeled, one or both begin to feel anxious or bored, as though something is lacking. That restlessness triggers aggravation, and before long, a break-up occurs.

Pretty soon, this pattern repeats itself. Two people meet and quickly fall in love. Things move quickly, and sex takes place early in the relationship. But again, once those wildly-in-love feelings begin to wane, one or both begin to feel anxious or bored, and before long, the relationship breaks up.

Sometimes a couple will stay together simply because they do not want to be alone, but all the while they feel empty and hollow inside. Neither one knows why it is like it is or what to do about it.

As we grow up, we are hurt by others. It is a fact of life. Sometimes the hurts are small; other times they are huge. If we do not learn how to acknowledge that we were hurt, and if we do not learn how to deal with our pain, we do not learn how to have good relationships. Our lives will be shallow and hollow and empty.

Hurting people often hurt others. Not that they want to, or that they necessarily start their day looking for ways to hurt someone else, but like Emily, who felt as though she was disposable, they do not know how to handle their own hurts, let alone someone else's. So they back off, throw away relationships, and find themselves alone time and time again.

In cases like this, it is very scary to let down your guard, become vulnerable, and get close to someone. To do that involves trust, and if you do not have trust in someone, you do not have a good starting point for a relationship.

Before long, you will find that you are only attracting people like yourself; those who are non-committal; those who also hurt and are not willing to be vulnerable; those who think of you as disposable!

What kind of relationships do you have now? What kind of relationships do you want to have tomorrow? Relationships can be like fine China if you're willing to be open and vulnerable and committed for the long-haul; or your relationships can be like paper plates—easily bent, disposable, and good only for the short-term.

OVERLAPPING CIRCLES: A VIDEO GAME

This game begins with circles moving randomly around the screen. The goal is to get two of them to connect and to completely overlap so that they look like one circle. Many obstacles continually get in the way, making the game very difficult to win. Points are earned as the player gets the circles to overlap more.

In the game, Circle A and Circle B are attached most of the time, but, a lot like people, it seems they sometimes want to be apart. Even as they overlap more and more, they are still two separate circles.

Once they make a commitment to be together for the duration, they begin trying to become as one, but no matter how hard they try, they simply cannot make it happen. As time goes on, the struggle becomes more difficult so they decide to be apart from each other more often. Finally, they conclude there is no hope of ever being perfectly aligned and becoming as one so they simply give up the struggle. To their amazement, they then find themselves moving naturally into the overlapping position without even trying.

The overlapping feels good, and as it continues, it becomes even more comfortable. Now they are traveling around the screen together as one, content, not looking like two attached circles, or two circles stacked one on top of the other, or two separate circles, but two happily overlapping circles.

APPLICATION

Relationships

EXPLANATION

Before two people meet and fall in love, they are singles who like to hang out with other singles and do their own thing. They are like the circles in the story, moving around, trying to connect with other circles.

Once two people find someone they enjoy talking and becoming acquainted with, they spend time together, discovering their similarities as well as their differences.

During this time, they don't mind the differences, and may even find each other's flaws to be humorous or virtuous. As in the analogy, the two circles attach to each other quite often, but allow each other to have their differences and their space.

Once the couple gets married, they become a family—one unit consisting of two individuals. Because their new family is unlike their own family of origin, they may each start judging the other and become critical. The husband may complain, expecting his wife to think and act like he does.

Take Anthony and Susie for example. Anthony's mother stayed at home and took care of the kids and the household chores. This was her full-time job, and she kept everything spotless, neat, and tidy. When his father came home from work, there was never any housework for him to do, and the rules were established that the home was her job and earning money was his.

Susie, on the other hand, was brought up in a home where both parents worked, and they shared the household responsibilities without question or discussion. They worked together toward the common goal of taking care of the daily chores.

When Anthony and Susie got married, they had different expectations. Anthony expected Susie to take care of the house, and it never occurred to him to help out. On the other hand, Susie assumed that he would help with chores as soon as he came home from work, and she expected to not have to ask him.

Their expectations were contrary to each other, and this quickly became a major source of contention.

When Susie asked for his help, Anthony either complained that she was nagging or simply ignored her requests. This made her very angry.

Anthony was angry, too, because Susie's housekeeping fell far short of his mother's. He thought she should understand that it was very important to him to have a flawless home.

It was true that Susie's housekeeping was different from his mother's, but it looked good enough to her. She thought he was too picky and a perfectionist; he thought she was lax and expected him to do "her job."

The war was on, and they each wanted the other to change. They each wanted the home they were brought up in, but it simply couldn't happen because they were not the same people as their parents. They were unique individuals with different tastes and priorities. They could not change each other; it was impossible.

Remember in the analogy how the two circles tried to align perfectly? They wanted to change each other so they would be exactly alike. Trying to change your partner just will not work. Arguing will likely happen; maybe one will give the silent treatment while the other slams doors. However each responds, it will be important to give the other some space—some time apart to cool down and think.

Going to counseling helped Anthony and Susie to realize that they are different and cannot force the other to change. They needed to let go of unreasonable expectations and come up with a plan that worked for their own family. They made a list of the household chores and they each "signed up" for chores for which they would be responsible. They also agreed to clean the house together on Saturday mornings and afterwards go out and do something fun together. In this manner, they grew closer and began to better understand each other's needs.

This is like the analogy. When Circle A and Circle B stopped trying to force their overlapping, the more they let go and enjoyed each other, the closer they became, and the overlapping area became larger.

How does a couple enlarge the overlapping in their marriage? Following are several ways to develop common ground:

Social Common Ground: Make common friends by joining a couple's Bible study group; participate in the same church ministries; attend a social or business interest group; take classes together. It is not necessary to give up the healthy friendships you had prior to getting married; in fact, it is important to maintain them. (Those that are unhealthy must be given up.) Likewise, it is important to develop friendships with other couples to enjoy together.

Common Interests and Activities: Explore the activities that you each like. You might discover that you enjoy the same ones. Try others too, such as bike riding, walking in the woods, playing sports, traveling, taking a dance class, putting together a puzzle, playing a table game, going to see a movie, dining out, attending a musical. The more you discover your common interests, the more you will enjoy your time together.

Spiritual Common Ground: Spending time together reading the Bible and praying helps couples stay together. Praying with and for each other strengthens your relationship with God and each other. It is important to note how prayers are answered: yes, no, or wait. Life becomes more manageable and enjoyable knowing your partner is riding alongside you on life's roller coaster, while God holds you both securely in His hand.

Emotional Common Ground: Make it safe to share feelings with each other. This is an important ingredient to keep the marriage together. Be a good listener; do not interrupt and interject your own opinion. You are not really listening when you are thinking of what you are going to say next. Doing so will shut off the communication because the speaker does not feel he is being understood or respected.

When necessary, set a timer and allow each person to talk at least ten to fifteen minutes. While the speaker is talking, the listener listens intently without interruption. This can eliminate assumptions and misunderstandings. God gives us two ears and one mouth to remind us to listen more and talk less!

Physical Common Ground: Once two people get married, they become exclusive to each other. It is not a good idea for a married man or woman to be alone with a person of the opposite sex, even if they are longtime friends. Not allowing yourself to meet alone with someone of the opposite sex will stop rumors before they have the chance to start! It is very easy for a male-female relationship to cross the fine line between friendship and intimacy, and you could easily find yourself involved in an inappropriate relationship, i.e. an affair. By setting strong boundaries as a couple, you will develop trust, which is the single most important ingredient in any relationship.

Sexual Common Ground: Sexual relationships should be limited to the couple themselves. Any sexual relationship outside of a marriage destroys it.

The more common ground you can establish with your mate makes the overlapping of circles larger, causing your relationship to grow ever deeper.

HOW BIG IS YOUR PIECE OF THE PIE?

Spending quality time in a marriage is like a cutting a pie. When you first get married, the pie is divided into only two parts—husband and wife. They can have quality and quantity time together because there are only two people. As the family grows attention goes mainly to the children, and the couple can hardly find any time to be alone together.

The family in the following story has six children, so their pie has eight slices (two parents and six kids). Besides the kids, there are many other responsibilities to tend to, all of which take another slice out of the pie. This type of lifestyle can leave a couple emotionally drained and detached from one another.

Does this sound familiar to you?

APPLICATION

Managing quality time in family and marriage

The Hippo That Fell Off the Seesaw

Explanation

Jodi and Jeff were newlyweds and very much in love. They texted each other at work and could hardly wait 'til evening to be together again. Life was light, fun, and full of joy. On weekends they played in the kitchen, testing new recipes and laughing at some of the concoctions they came up with. One of their favorite things to make was pie. While Jeff made his out-of-this-world killer crust, Jodi prepared various fillings by shaving white and dark chocolate, chopping cherries, and grating lemon rinds. Their specialty was lemon meringue, but they enjoyed the challenge of trying all sorts of new pie recipes.

When the pie was done, they would take it into the living room and eat it right out of the pan. Mmmm. They had such a good time eating, talking, watching TV, and snuggling together.

Because they wanted to someday have a large family, they lived on Jeff's income and put Jodi's into savings. They patiently waited for the time when their dreams would become a reality.

Two years went by until they learned they were expecting their first child. Excitement filled their thoughts as they decorated the baby's room, considered names, shopped for baby clothes, and discussed how they would raise their little one. The baby was named Joe, and he was a roly-poly little guy with a huge smile and a dimple in his chin. Lots of hullabaloo surrounded the family, what with all the picture-taking, relatives visiting, and showing him off to everyone.

With the baby's arrival, Jeff and Jodi's time and energy was now divided. No longer were they able to think only of what they wanted to do because now Joey's needs and wants were put ahead of their own. They continued to bake and experiment with pies, but not quite as often; and now there were three to share the pie so Jeff and Jodi's portions were a bit smaller.

Johnny, baby number two, arrived two years later; and once again time, attention, and energy was divided. Joey loved his little brother, and the family enjoyed this season of life. When Jeff came home from work, dinner was ready; and often the boys would have picked a bouquet of dandelions for daddy and mommy. A nighttime routine was established, and Jeff and Jodi enjoyed some time together after the kids were put to bed.

Now there were two little helpers to roll out pie crust, and instead of three to share the pie, there were four—still plenty enough to go around, just not as much of it.

Jimmy arrived next, and the household seemed to explode with energy. The schedule stayed about the same, but now when the kids went to bed, so did Jeff and Jodi. They didn't spend time alone anymore talking or baking, and it seemed that they didn't have much else to talk about other than the children. Because of the busyness, they didn't even realize that they were at a dangerous point in their marriage.

Baby number four was a beautiful girl named Jill, a little darling with reddish hair and hazel eyes. Jodi had fun shopping garage sales and second-hand stores for dresses and pink panties and socks with ruffles. The boys took quickly to their little sister and protected her fiercely from outsiders.

Over the years, home-baked pies became a tradition and a family affair. With six people now each having a slice, the dessert didn't go nearly as far as it used to, but because the time together was so enjoyable, no one seemed to mind.

Twins Jackie and Janet arrived next, filling the house to the brim. Resources were stretched to the max, and desserts became a rare treat. Sometimes on a Sunday night, Jeff would roll up his sleeves and bake one of his favorite pies, and the aroma would waft throughout the house, bringing smiles of anticipation to everyone. Now there were eight people (six children and two parents) sharing one pie, and it was necessary that each piece be carefully cut; after all, it would be a crime indeed if one child's piece of the pie was larger than another's! There was the same delicious taste, but oh boy, those slices sure seemed downright skimpy now.

And like the slices of pie, Jodi's and Jeff's time, attention, and energy were also divided eight ways. About ninety-five percent of their time was devoted to the six children, with the remaining five percent spent with each other or for each to have a minute or two all alone. If Jodi was lucky, she would be able to take a bath without interruption; if Jeff was lucky, he would spend a little time reading his favorite book without someone climbing on him. Jodi was almost always too tired for sex, plus she felt inhibited because she didn't want the children to hear any noise they might make.

For the most part, Jodi and Jeff were content and accepting of this new and busy life they had created. Unwittingly, though, they had also created a huge problem. By not recognizing their need to nurture their marriage, and by not spending adequate time alone with each other, they ended up with almost nothing in common except the children.

How about you? Have you found that you and your spouse almost never spend time together to just enjoy each other?

In the beginning, Jeff and Jodi had as much time together as they wanted after work and on weekends. They had the whole pie to themselves, so to speak. It was fun discovering new things about each other, doing whatever they wanted, and being carefree. They were secure and content in their connected little world. Time and money were abundant and other cares were not yet imposed upon them.

With the birth of their first baby, they experienced a dividing of all their resources—time, attention, money, and interests. Instead of each having half the pie, it was now cut into thirds. The baby needed both parents and the division was a naturally-occurring process. Those precious resources were divided again and again with the arrival of each successive child, until there was nothing left for Jodi and Jeff as a couple. Could they realistically afford to do anything apart from their children? Everyone with children understands that good child-care givers are expensive and hard to find, and family members don't necessarily want to be infringed upon. What is the solution?

At the beginning, a family is made of two parts—husband and wife. They can spend quality time together. As they began to have more children, each child will represent one more part. The needs of each part (child) are multifaceted—physical, spiritual, emotional, social, and financial. Each must be nurtured in order to thrive. A healthy marriage is the foundation, or the basis, of a healthy family. There cannot be a healthy family without a healthy and strong foundation, or marriage, on which to build.

What happened in Jodi's and Jeff's case is nothing new. With children demanding their time and energy, they ignored their own needs and their needs as a couple. When those needs are ignored, the foundation of the family is jeopardized. This is often the point at which either the husband or the wife become vulnerable to an affair, getting in trouble with money, or consuming too much alcohol or prescription drugs. A person whose needs are not met at home may look elsewhere to get them fulfilled.

Here are some practical ways to strengthen your marriage and keep it fun:

- Allow for individual alone time. Each person needs time to away from everyone else to read, be quiet, take a walk, or enjoy a hobby. Make sure you and your spouse each does something enjoyable every once in a while.
- Spend time together as a couple doing something you both like. At this point, you are not allowed to talk about problems, but only things you find interesting, funny, or relaxing. Date nights keep a couple connected and stable. Make plans well in advance and preserve that time.
- Learn to laugh again. Find fun in the silliness. Don't act your age; act your kids' age! Rediscover life and see things again for the first time.
- Find fun things to do that don't cost anything. A new job took Sherry and Jerry and their children to Washington State to live, miles away from their families. They had little money so they enjoyed walking and sight-seeing. One day they passed an

apple tree in a city lot, bearing much fruit. When they realized that those perfectly good apples were going to waste, they took off their jackets and used them to carry as many apples as possible. Back home in their kitchen, they busied themselves peeling, coring, and slicing them. By day's end, they had made an apple pie and a batch of apple jelly. The next day they went back and did it all over again, but this time they took paper sacks with them! Those free apples provided them with a fun time in the kitchen doing something they loved.

- Prepare for the unexpected. You never know where you will find a treasure, even something as simple as apples. These times will provide you with the much-needed laughter and playfulness your heart desires. Buy a kite and fly it in an empty field. Pack up the family along with a loaf of bread and a package of bologna and picnic in a public park. Go swimming at a lake or public pool. Get an ice cream cone for everyone and walk while eating it. Help the kids set up a lemonade stand by the sidewalk.

Using your time wisely is similar to intentionally cutting your pie. By planning ahead, you decide how much you will have and how it will be used. Otherwise, the decision will be made <u>for</u> you and you won't have any idea where it all went.

Marriage starts with two and ends with two because children are only in your house for a short time. Nurturing your marriage along the way ensures that a happy and healthy relationship will continue well after you become empty-nesters.

In other words, if you're careful, you could have your pie and eat it too!

THE PUSHY BULLDOZER AND WIMPY SOIL

Have you ever watched a bulldozer at work? It digs deep into the earth and removes a huge mass all at once, then turns and dumps it out nearby. This happens over and over again until a mountain of soil has been moved. Then the dozer begins pushing and flattening the dirt until it is properly graded and ready for a building project.

The bulldozer and the earth could be likened to a co-dependent relationship, with the soil being the person who is easily manipulated, and the dozer being the one who manipulates.

The following story is a perfect example of this. Alicia is a people pleaser, easily pushed around and manipulated like the soil. Her sister, Debbie, is like the dozer, doing whatever it takes to get her own way.

APPLICATION

Co-dependent relationships

EXPLANATION

Alicia enjoyed sewing and was, in fact, a talented seamstress. One day while browsing the fabric shop, she came upon a bolt of fabric that was so lovely, it took her aback. Not only were the colors just the right mix but the material itself would sew well and fray little. She bought the entire four yards and showed it to her sister, Debbie, as soon as she got home. Alicia was a frugal young lady, and although she did not yet have definite plans for the fabric, she had decided to save it for a special purpose.

Debbie also thought the fabric was gorgeous and wondered what she herself could use it for. Knowing that Alicia had purchased the bolt end and there was no more like it in the store, Debbie reasoned that it was only fair for her to have some of it, too.

If she "borrowed" only a small strip, perhaps she could make her daughter a headband. *Certainly Alicia wouldn't mind sharing a small amount*, she thought. So she asked, and Alicia gladly complied. The headband looked darling on the little girl with bouncy, golden curls.

Still, Debbie was not content and wondered what else she could do with Alicia's precious fabric. By this point, Debbie was consumed with having it all, and even justified ways to get it. She thought of the worn pillows on her couch and how that fabric would be perfect for pillow covers. She went to her sister again, and asked if she could "borrow" a yard.

Alicia loved her sister, but it seemed that there was always tension between them. She never took the time to assess the relationship so she didn't understand the problem. She was annoyed with Debbie, but she thought that if she said no, there would be a family feud, so she begrudgingly handed over the fabric. She consoled herself with the fact that there were still almost three yards left, enough to make a stunning dress for her husband's upcoming work party, or maybe even something else. She still wasn't sure yet what she wanted to sew, but there was no hurry. She held the material on her lap and felt its texture. Smooth and soft, not given to wrinkles and would hold its shape and drape nicely. She was thankful there was still enough left to do something with.

Meanwhile, Debbie took the yard of fabric and sewed two perky pillow covers, which indeed brightened up the couch. Knowing there were still almost three yards left, Debbie was already conjuring up ways to justify getting the rest of the fabric for herself. She was determined she would have that remaining fabric if it was the last thing she did.

Again she approached Alicia, asking for the remainder for a skirt for her daughter's rehearsal. And wouldn't it be perfect with the headband! Alicia seethed at the request but caved in as usual and handed it over without saying a word. Once Debbie left, Alicia cried and cried. Not only had she given up her entire purchase, she was sick and tired of being bullied by Debbie. Feelings of hatred welled up inside her, and she thought of a few choice things to say next time Debbie came around.

This was not the way Alicia wanted to live, and she could feel herself slipping further into depression. A lifetime of giving in was about to tear Alicia apart, but she didn't know what to do. In all of her relationships, it seemed, she was the one to give in. An angry fire burned in her belly as she recalled the countless times she had let others have their way while she got nothing in return. On the other hand, Debbie seemed to always get her way. With her parents, her family, and her friends, she was the one who always came out on top, with no thought of what anyone else might be feeling.

One day Alicia decided to get some help from a Christian counselor to learn how to deal effectively with her sister. She learned that the reason she was depressed was because she did not enforce her boundaries. This surprised Alicia because she did not even know she had boundaries. The counselor assured her that even though she may not fully understand what her boundaries are, she does have them, and when they are violated, she will experience feelings of violation, loss, anger, hopelessness, and hurt, which will culminate in a sense of depression. Alicia learned how to establish and enforce boundaries by thinking of past situations and how she wished she had handled them; then she thought ahead of what would be the proper response to similar events. She learned how and when to say yes or no and she practiced saying no with her counselor until she was comfortable.

The next time Debbie came over and asked for something, Alicia was more prepared. Changing behavior can take a long time, but Alicia was determined. Imagine the surprise when Debbie did not get her own way. She stomped off and went home, but secretly she knew her sister was right. Over time she gained a great deal of respect for Alicia, who in turn felt very good about her newly-found territorial rights.

Today the sisters have a much healthier relationship and interact as adults should. With Alicia's firmly rooted boundaries, they can discuss topics that before would have been off-limits and caused fights. Through all of this, Debbie is learning that some of her own behavior is unhealthy, and Alicia is secretly hoping that Debbie will someday get help for herself. Alicia now has peace and joy, and establishing boundaries is something she wishes she had done long ago. She is more confident and caring, and her faith walk has become deeper as well.

You see, God sets boundaries with us all the time, but we often fail to recognize them. Once we get a fresh, godly perspective, it is easier for us to establish boundaries in our lives.

TURTLE PEOPLE

Sometimes turtles like to hide their heads inside their shell. If you pick up a turtle and talk to it, more than likely he'll quickly hide his head inside where you cannot see. You might try coaxing him out of his shell by knocking on it, bribing him with food, talking sweetly, or poking him with a stick, but the more you try, the more determined he may be to stay away from you.

You could end up feeling downright frustrated because that darned old turtle will not cooperate no matter what!

The truth is, if you wait patiently for the turtle to come out on his own terms, sooner or later, he will.

APPLICATION

Human relationships

EXPLANATION

Often in relationships there is a pursuer—the one who wants attention—and there is a withdrawer, or the turtle, the one who is being coaxed to give attention. The pursuer tries to get the withdrawer out of his shell, so to speak, to talk, listen, or play. But sometimes the turtle person is shy and doesn't feel comfortable just being natural and letting things happen. And the more the pursuer pushes, the more the withdrawer withdraws, just like a turtle who tucks himself deep within his shell.

But if the pursuer will simply leave the "turtle person" alone for a while and give him some space, eventually the turtle person will stick his head out and respond. It may take a while, but turtle people can't hide in their shells forever. Once the turtle person feels safe, he or she might even become the pursuer in that relationship!

Parent-Child

Mom thinks her daughter, Suzy, is having a problem. She tries to get Suzy to open up and talk, but she will end up very frustrated if Suzy isn't ready and doesn't respond. Parents often feel that because they've been through life's hard times, their children will automatically trust them with secrets and innermost feelings, but such is not often the case, no matter how "hip" a parent may be. The generation gap is just as real today as it always has been. A child needs to know for certain that he or she is safe to talk, and that what is said will not be mocked or looked down upon. Under the right circumstances a conversation can flourish.

One day George was concerned that his son, Joe, had things on his mind and needed to talk. George hinted around a few times but without success. Joe was in his teens and had a girlfriend, but he was beginning to withdraw from his dad and from his friends. Concerned, George took the initiative to plan a fishing outing with the just the two of them on an upcoming Sunday afternoon. He let Joe know enough time in advance so as not to cause problems in his schedule, and when the time came, the two set off for the lake.

The weather conditions were less than ideal for fishing, but since fishing was not George's ultimate goal, he didn't let it create a problem. Out on the lake, the two were able to relax. George never broached any subjects, but let God do the work. In time, Joe began to open up to his dad about some things that were on his mind.

George was a wise father. He looked for and arranged a safe place where he and Joe could be alone to talk, and when the time was right, he backed off and waited for his boy to open up to him.

Marriage

If you are trying to get your spouse's attention, be careful! Going about it in the wrong manner can backfire in the same way that prodding a turtle with a stick doesn't work. If your spouse's natural tendency is to withdraw, you can wind up feeling frustrated and very, very lonely. Sometimes the loneliest place to be is with someone who doesn't share your interests.

If you are in that situation, don't lose heart. Instead of trying to get your sweetheart's attention, go to God and focus on Him. He has awesome attributes and is waiting to share them with you. God knows all about that emptiness and hurt inside you, and He wants to fill it with His love and healing grace. He is waiting to put His strong arms around you and hold you tightly.

You know how you want to share things with your spouse? Well, God has things He wants to share with you, too. Once you let God fill up that void, you will be less needy and less demanding on your soul mate.

It is truly a wonderful bonus when our spouse meets some of our emotional needs, but God is the only one who can meet all of them.

Great things happen when we direct our efforts toward pursuing God. First and foremost, it brings us closer to Him and allows us to experience the joy and peace that only He can give. Once that happens, our need for the attention of others begins to diminish. In turn, our spouse is relieved from the pressure to be at our beck and call and then they, too, can experience some freedom to open up to you.

RELATIONAL CIRCLE

Have you ever felt as though you just don't quite fit in anywhere? Perhaps you've felt that way at church or at work, or even hanging out with your friends. To feel accepted, you might try to impress others by boasting of your accomplishments, by one-upping everyone with better stories or funnier jokes, or by trying to be the life of the party.

But no matter what you do, those tactics usually don't work. In the end, you still end up frustrated and lonely and feeling somewhat like a square peg trying to fit into a round hole.

There is a popular computer game called Relational Circle. The game consists of seven circles placed in the center of one another, with space around each. Every circle represents a town, and the smallest, inner circle belongs to you, and that one is called Popularity Town.

Walking randomly around the large outer circle are thousands of people. The object of the game is to pull as many people as possible into your town and then keep them there.

This is a game of speed, and the player has only a few seconds in which to lock onto a person and bring him in. If you aren't fast enough, the computer will grab him away and place him in another town. The more people in a town, the larger and more popular that town becomes. And once you lose someone, you cannot go back and try for that person again; you have to go back to the very outside edge and start all over again.

At the end of the game, the town with the most people is deemed the most popular, and a mayor is appointed. Hopefully that will be Popularity Town, and if it is, you will become the mayor. The game can be quite intense, and players often feel tense, almost panicky in their venture of getting as many people into their town as possible. Sometimes their failure to do so leaves them quite frustrated.

Does this game sound like fun to you, or does it sound silly? Or does it perhaps hit a little close to home?

Many of us are living our lives in a fashion very similar to that game—desperately and frantically trying to be popular, to get as many friends as possible. We not only want to be popular, we want to be the most popular and the most well-liked. In reality, however, just the opposite is often true. When we are desperate for friendships, they often elude us, and we may find ourselves frustrated, angry sometimes aggressively pursuing the companionship of others.

The truth is, people are not going to like us all of the time. Why not? Because God made you and me, and everyone else in the whole world, uniquely individual! He gave us different families and ethnic backgrounds, different personalities and different talents, different smells, thoughts, tastes, different likes and dislikes. He uses each of us in interesting ways for His own glory and purpose.

Life is not a game, but indeed it is a design organized by God Himself. And like the game, whether or not you are aware of it, you place each of your friends and acquaintances into one of four circles—Intimate, Relational, Casual, and Acquaintances. How you categorize someone has everything to do with your past, how you see things, how you feel about things, and all of those wonderful unique characteristics God placed within your individualized makeup.

The Intimate Circle

This is the smallest, innermost circle and is reserved solely for very close friends, those you trust implicitly with secrets and feelings. Here you are free to reveal pain, disappointments, and fears; successes, joys, blessings, and hopes.

Not everyone has an intimate friend with whom to share, so blessed indeed are those who do. Seldom does a person have more than three intimate friends throughout the span of a lifetime. These relationships are sacred treasures and should be highly regarded.

The Close Circle

This circle is somewhat larger, and the people here are referred to as close friends. You see and talk to these folks most often and share many things with them. They know most of your family stories, most of your concerns, and maybe even most of your dreams. These people are near and dear to your heart, and you love them and value their friendship; however, you do not feel free to share with them your innermost secrets, which are reserved for your intimate friends.

The Casual Circle

Casual friends belong in the third circle, which is larger still than the other two. You see and interact with these people once in a while, at special events, neighborhood get-togethers, or at church on Sunday mornings. The conversations are somewhat superficial and guarded, and they may include topics such as the weather, the economy, or the latest in clothing trends. When people talk about their families, they are likely to tell all of the success stories and none of the painful, personal details.

The Acquaintance Circle

Everyone else falls into the large outer circle of acquaintances. You see these folks occasionally, perhaps in the hallway at work or on the elevator, but you have little if anything to talk about. When you do, the depth of conversation may be no more than a quick, "Hello, how are you doing?"

APPLICATION

Tension can be created in any circle when you try to be a people pleaser and force others into your circle of intimacy. Remember, not everyone wants a deep level of intimacy. If you detect even the least amount of resistance, back off and let that person have the space he needs. An intimate friendship may develop someday, but it will never happen when forced.

Remember that not everyone has to be your friend, nor do you have to be everybody else's friend. You determine into which circle of friendship to place your friends. The level of friendship changes all the time. An intimate friend may decide not to be close to you anymore; that is okay because you can put her into the outer circle as causal friends. You are in charge of the circle, and you decide where to put everyone.

Inner peace and relational peace come from realizing that it is okay and necessary to have friends in every circle. An even greater level of inner peace comes from knowing that God is in control, and He specifically created you for His purposes. He has a plan for you. He knows your every thought and weakness and strength, and He loves you unconditionally in spite of yourself.

Letting go of the worry of whether or not you are liked or accepted by others is a key factor in gaining inner freedom.

SELF-IMAGE/SELF-ESTEEM

GROUP PHOTO

Long-time friends Jeannie, Anita, Kerry, and Mandy went on a vacation together to Europe. For almost a year they had planned and plotted and struggled to save enough money for the trip. Excitement filled the air when the big day came and they boarded the plane.

The first destination was Great Britain, and from there it was to Paris by train. They thrilled at the hustle and bustle of the fast-paced city life, and once they almost got lost on the crowded, narrow streets and one-way alleys. In the tranquility of the beautiful countryside, they couldn't help but praise God for creating such a masterpiece.

And, of course, they took pictures everywhere they went. There were pictures of sheep grazing in pastures lined with miles and miles of stone walls, pictures of hidden waterfalls and out-of-the way shops, of castles lying in ruins, and of bicyclers weaving in and out of city traffic. They took group photos and pictures of each other caught off-guard making funny faces.

When the trip came to an end and the foursome returned home, they were exhausted, happy, and full of tales to tell. When they got together a week later at Jeannie's house, they shared pictures and talked about their adventures. Photo after photo was brought out, and each woman excitedly looked for herself in every one. Sometimes they didn't even bother to look at their friends' photos because they were only interested in how they appeared.

Each woman was equally guilty. Jeannie fussed that her hair was unkempt, while Anita swore that she really wasn't as fat as she looked.

Kerry detested the shadow created by her nose and Mandy insisted that the light made her skin look pasty.

This is a good example of how self-centered people really can be!

APPLICATION

Low self-esteem, shyness, low self-image, eating disorders

EXPLANATION

Tina is a thirty-two-year-old woman with a negative view of herself due to her weight. When she saw two of her co-workers talking to each other in the hall one day, Tina jumped to the conclusion that they were making fun of her body. She swallowed her tears and felt very hurt. Later two other co-workers were in a deep discussion, and when she walked by they stopped talking and smiled at her. She imagined they were also talking badly about her and thinking that she looked disgusting. In reality, however, all of her co-workers were generally selfish people who were not thinking about her at all, but instead were thinking about themselves. They were like the women in the story who only cared about themselves.

Anna, twenty-three, weighed ninety-five pounds soaking wet and thought that she was overweight. She had trouble eating in public because she thought others were carefully watching how much she ate and what types of food she ate.

They must think I eat like a pig when I consume most everything on my plate, she told herself over and over. So in order to avoid the imagined judgment, Anna could barely swallow any food at all. The reality, however, was that no one paid any attention to what she ate because they were all too busy making sure their own stomachs were full! Like the women in the story, the people in the restaurant only cared how they themselves were perceived. Due to her unfounded insecurities, Anna spent her days thinking of how people watched her eat whenever she was in public.

Barb was very shy and afraid to be with people. When she worked outside in the yard, she worried that her neighbor would come over and talk to her and that she would have nothing of interest to say. When she passed someone in the hall at work, she thought she was being scrutinized and judged for her appearance.

Barb's worst nightmare was at Bible study when she could not come up with anything to say. She was certain everyone in the group thought that she was weird. The truth was, no one paid attention to her because they were too busy minding their own business.

How many of us go through life worrying about how others see us? Truthfully, everyone else is too busy to think about you. How many stressful hours, days, or even years, have you wasted worrying that others are judging you while all the time they are not?

MIRROR, MIRROR ON THE WALL

Mirror, mirror on the wall, who's the fairest of them all? Deep within the secret place of our hearts, where no one can see, we each desire to be the "fairest of them all." Maybe we would deny it; maybe we would admit it. But what happens to us when we discover that we are indeed among the *unfairest* of them all?

Beth went into the room to look in the mirror. It had been years since she'd seen her own image. She was youthful then. She had a twinkle in her eye, shiny black hair, and pep in her step. Seeing that beautiful young girl again would assure herself that she was still at the top of the heap, so to speak.

But time had passed, and the image looking back at her was that of a much older woman whose face now sported droopy eyes; wrinkles around her mouth; dull, graying hair; and a large age spot on her cheek. As Beth stared into the mirror, an unbearable pain settled into her heart.

Later that same day, Allison went in to see her reflection in the mirror. Like Beth, it had been years since she'd seen her own image and she, too, expected to see that young, beautiful girl with golden hair, fair skin, a sparkle in her eye, and a perky smile. How cute she had been!

When she held the mirror to her face, however, she gasped with horror. Instead of youthful beauty, she saw wrinkles and graying hair, dark circles under her eyes, a chipped tooth, droopy eyelids, and a few hairs growing from places they didn't belong! She stared at her image for a long time before leaving with a sinking feeling of distress.

Both Beth and Allison were changed forever by the harsh reality of what they saw.

How did that mirror, that thin piece of glass, hold such power over those who looked into it? Did it reflect only the outside of the person, or did it reveal something deeper, something not seen with human eyes?

Application

Self-image

Explanation

When Beth and Allison looked into the mirror, they were rather horrified at what they saw. Why? Because they had always pictured themselves as young beauties untouched by time. They highly valued their good looks and smirked at those who were less than beautiful. Shock and disappointment awaited them, but something else was also at work here.

A person's character lies deep within, unseen, hidden from view. Now that Beth and Allison's human flaws were revealed, their true characters emerged.

Here is what happened and how each woman reacted to her own reality.

Beth

Beth went home, brokenhearted and empty because her beauty was no more. She convinced herself that no one would want to be friends with her because of perceived ugliness. She told herself she'd never be able to find a man to love her and that she needed to give up the idea of ever having a family of her own.

She withdrew from her friends and family and left the house only to go to work and run necessary errands. As much as possible, she avoided all social contact.

Beth had always placed a very high value on outward appearances, and now her world was ripped apart. She felt that life was no longer worth living, and she wanted to die. She became a recluse, self-absorbed in her own pity, and as time passed, she grew even more unsightly because she loathed herself.

Allison

The image of that old woman in the mirror haunted Allison for days. Try as she may, she could not banish it from her mind's eye. She longed to regain some of that beauty, as well as the playfulness and carefree attitude she used to have. Like Beth, Allison entertained awful thoughts of how she was negatively perceived by others and of how no man would possibly ever want such a homely woman.

But one day Allison decided she was not going to stay at that pity party any more. Instead she would find some someone to help her become the fun person she really wanted to be.

She found a Christian counselor and made an appointment to talk things over. She needed a positive outside perspective—someone

The Hippo That Fell Off the Seesaw

who would tell her the truth, challenge her, and help her focus on the changes necessary to reach her new goals.

The counselor told her that the Bible says in Psalms that she was fearfully and wonderfully made. She also told her about Christ and all He had done for her on the cross. Not yet understanding it fully, Allison accepted it as truth and accepted Christ as her Savior. Immediately she began to feel inner peace she'd not known before.

New confidence and renewed energy began to build within Allison. She started taking short walks after work. At first she was nervous about people looking at her, but then she noticed that they were waving as she passed by, and her confidence grew.

Allison felt as though she was discovering a brand new world. She began to fall in love with her life, and made even more discoveries. She found that she actually liked some of the healthy foods she hadn't tried before and that she enjoyed cleaning her house—something she had not spent much time doing before. She took up embroidery in the winter and gardening in the summer.

The very best addition to Allison's life was her new relationship with Christ. He filled the empty place in her heart, and she learned that all the things she'd been missing before stemmed from that deep void. Knowing Jesus as Savior gave purpose to her life. Many times, she told her friends, "Now that I've got something worth dying for, life really is worth living!" Her friends could not dismiss the new vitality and love that exuded from her.

CONCLUSION

Like Beth and Allison, you also view yourself as being or looking a certain way. Perhaps your self-perception is accurate, and what you see really is how things are. Or, like the women we just read about, perhaps you look at life through rose-colored glasses, and when reality sets in, it throws you for a loop.

How we see ourselves can either immobilize us with fear or grief, or motivate us to change for the better. Are you like Beth, or are you like Allison? How you respond is entirely up to you.

Beth looked inside herself and, finding no resources from which to draw, spent the rest of her life wallowing in self-pity, much like a pig stuck in the mire. What a shameful waste.

Allison used negative self-image as motivation to change. When she looked within, she was wise enough to realize that she did not have the wherewithal to help herself. What did she do? She ran for her life toward someone who could help her!

When you look at your life, how do you respond? Do you wallow in pity or do you run for help?

THE SENSITIVE PLANT *(MIMOSA PUDICA)*

Ding! Ding! Ding! What a joyful sound for the school children because it signals time for recess. Being confined in the classroom is torture for most children; they cannot wait to run outside and play.

On the playground of Childrenville Elementary School in Hawaii, children were swinging on the swings, climbing on the jungle gym, and playing soccer. Some were sitting in groups talking. Playground supervisors were trying to stop a fight between two boys. But three little girls—Lisa, Lauren, and Emmy—were busy occupying themselves with a *Mimosa pudica*, commonly called a sensitive plant. A sensitive plant has leafy ferns, which are normally fully extended for maximum light absorption. When touched, however, the leaves immediately fold up and are barely discernable.

Lisa touched a plant and watched in delight as the leaves quickly closed up. Lauren followed suit, laughing out loud as the leaves closed up. Emmy touched a third plant and squealed as the leaves closed up. While they were doing this, Lisa remarked, "Emmy, this plant reminds me of you because when people come close to you, your face turns red and you get frozen up." Emmy put her head down and smiled. While they searched for more sensitive plants, Lauren said, "Let's look for more Emmy plants!" The three giggled and laughed as they found and touched more sensitive plants. They seemed to be on a mission to touch every single plant on the playground before recess was over.

Later that night while Emmy lay on her bed thinking about her day, she began to sob. She hated being shy.

Why am I different from other people? I wish I could be like Lisa who is not afraid to say anything to anyone. Not only am I afraid of strangers; I'm even afraid to talk to my parents and my friends. Tears ran down her cheeks, and Emmy cried herself to sleep.

APPLICATION

Shyness, social anxiety

EXPLANATION

Shyness is a stumbling block to anyone, no matter what the person's age. It is not at all silly; it makes a person feel inferior and backward. Shyness causes people to avoid social situations, and can prevent career advancement. People are often mistakenly labeled as aloof, unfriendly, or stuck-up, when the truth is that they long to have close friendships. Shy people often admire extroverts, those who seem to have no fear of speaking up.

Left unchecked, a shy person can sink more deeply into despair or depression every day. Mira was exactly like Emmy when she was little. She was afraid to be with people. She felt awkward saying anything and felt that people would not like her. When she grew up, she was still shy. She avoided most social situations so she would not feel embarrassed.

If she knew she was going to talk to someone, she would rehearse the conversation over and over again in an effort to not say the wrong thing. While isolation seemed safe, she deeply longed to be accepted by her peers.

Mira was not born shy, but became that way out of self-defense. As a young child, her parents and grandparents expected a lot out of her. No matter how hard she tried, whatever she did was not good enough for them.

Mira's dad was a physically small, unsuccessful salesman. As a teenager, he was afraid to try out for sports because the other boys were so much bigger, and his cowardice caused him to become the laughing stock of the school. It seemed to Mira that he was trying to live through her by demanding that she excel in school as well as go out for sports even though she was not interested. Because she did not live up to what he wanted, she felt as if she was a failure in his eyes.

This feeling of unacceptance, unworthiness, permeated Mira's outlook on life. One time in the third grade, Mira volunteered to answer a question in front of the class but her answer was incorrect. She was terribly embarrassed. With that experience and all the rejection she was feeling at home, she vowed only to talk to others when it was absolutely necessary. She decided to make her world small and private and not let anyone in; that way she wouldn't make mistakes and be laughed at or ridiculed.

One time she made a comment to her friends and someone disagreed with her. Instead of accepting it for what it was, Mira took it personally and climbed back into her hole of silence. That private world took over Mira's life and she became utterly fearful. Instead of joining conversations, she pretended to not care. Others saw her as stuck-up and aloof and stayed away from her. Some people wondered if she was sad.

Although Mira made her world what it was, she still concluded that she was unlovable and that no one would ever like her. Loneliness, fatigue, and sadness were her only friends, and she avoided all social activities as much as possible.

One day, out of sheer desperation and with God's help, she gathered the courage to seek help through counseling with Dr. Rita. This was very difficult for Mira. What if even the counselor rejected her? What if Dr. Rita only verified Mira's worst fears? What would she do then? Nonetheless, she made the appointment and went in.

Dr. Rita welcomed her warmly and listened as Mira poured out her heart. Even though it was extremely difficult for her to talk, she was at the end of her rope and had reached out to her counselor as if she were a lifeline. As time passed, Mira learned that most of her trouble was with male authority figures, and that she avoided talking to her college professors and her boss at work. Dr. Rita pointed out that Mira interpreted all comments as criticism, whether or not they were, and offered godly wisdom and advice so Mira could overcome those bad thoughts, which are sometimes referred to as stinking thinking.

Over time, Mira began trusting Dr. Rita more and more, and tears became a regular part of the session. Tears are often a necessary part of the healing process. Mira learned to let go of the fear of rejection. She cried during many of the sessions as she talked about her past and the current struggles of being shy.

Eventually she was able to talk to her parents about her childhood pain. Because she followed Dr. Rita's advice and remained calm, she was able to have a healing conversation with her parents and grandparents, each of whom admitted that they had not understood how much their actions had affected her. They accepted their own flaws and apologized to her and to one another, and this opened a new door for their relationship to grow. Over time, Mira was finally able to leave the past behind. She accepted that she was not an outgoing person and that she did not need to try to be someone she was not. She also discovered that she was not the only person who struggled with shyness. In fact, she learned from Dr. Rita that 30–40 percent of all people struggle with that affliction. She came to accept herself. She was coached to smile at people to see their reactions. She realized that often they smiled back, and the world became a less fearful place.

She also came to realize that being a good listener was a gift. There are many people who need to talk and to have someone who will listen. Mira found that people liked to be with her because she would listen to their struggles.

She was challenged to smile more at people as she walked down the street. At first, she was nervous about acting so confident, but once she saw people smiling back at her, it became natural.

She had to accept the fact that everyone is entitled to their own opinions, whether or not they agree with her. Dr. Rita helped prepare Mira for when others had beliefs that were contrary to hers.

In social gatherings where she did not know anyone, she would look for someone who was sitting alone. She would approach that person, introduce herself, and made small talk. She would have prepared ahead of time questions to ask. She discovered that people like talking about themselves. This not only kept the conversation going; it helped keep the focus off of herself. As long as she was one-on-one, she was not self-conscious.

Further in her healing process, Dr. Rita encouraged Mira to open up to the people in her life. She took the chance and emailed one of her professors, explaining about her family background and why she was shy. Mira told the professor that from now on she would look him in the face and say hi every time she saw him in the hallway. From the time they had that conversation, the professor became more and more friendly and encouraged her to ask questions through email. Later on, she actually made appointments and met with the professors in person.

Dr. Rita helped her to see that there were not many "dads" in her world now—fewer people to threaten her and make her feel less than the wonderful person God made her to be. Her professor and her boss were not her dad.

Those words of wisdom and encouragement gave Mira the courage she needed to pursue relationships with her professors and her boss. Although Mira is still uncomfortable in groups, she is very good with one-on-one conversation. She has accepted herself the way God made her.

She took small steps to improve her social skills. She took risks and faced her insecurity. Mostly, the world is no longer a scary place for her.

Can you relate to any of the individuals in this book? Everyone experiences challenges, but the true ending of the story depends on how we handle each challenge. The analogies in this book portray difficult experiences in simple, tangible word pictures. God has worked through these stories to help change and heal the hearts of those who came for Christian counseling. Hopefully, you now have new insight into dealing with *your* challenges in life, improving *your* walk with God, dealing with *your* conflicts in an innovative way, maneuvering *your* relationships successfully, and improving *your* self-esteem. My prayer is that this book has motivated you to love God, others, and yourself more, so that you can be the person God called you to be. You are special and precious in God's sight!

—Dr. Rita

You may contact Dr. Rita through her email, dr.ritahuang@gmail.com, or visit her website at www.trinitychristiancounseling.com.

INDEX

Addiction, 63

Anger, 101, 128

Anxiety, 107, 121, 126

Bitterness, 128

Blaming, 37

Challenges, 13

Christian living, 41, 45, 57

Co-dependency, 173

Communication, 93

Conflict resolution, 83, 89, 93, 97, 101

Conversation, 93

Crises, 9

Dealing with sin, 40

Depression, 107, 121, 126

Eating disorders, 185

Faith in God, 21, 33

Forgiveness, 40

God's love, 21, 33

Gossip, 49

Grieving the loss of a pet, 117

Hidden sin, 63

Loneliness, 131

Making decisions, 52

Negative thoughts, 67

Perfectionism, 75

Quality time, 167

Relationships, 89, 137, 140, 144, 150, 163

    Adult-teen relationship, 158

    Friends, 179

    Husband-wife relationship, 148, 153, 176

    Parent-child relationship, 148, 176

Relationship with God, 25

Relaxation, 121

Self-image, 185, 187

Sexual addiction, 126

Shyness, 185, 191

Social anxiety, 191

Stress, 107, 111, 121

Time management, 167

Unforgiveness, 128

Unresolved conflict, 87

Victims of abuse, 72

Worry about the future, 45

www.ingramcontent.com/pod-product-compliance
Lightning Source LLC
LaVergne TN
LVHW051831080426
835512LV00018B/2823